Circle
of
Death

Clinton's Climb to the Presidency

by Richmond Odom

Huntington House Publishers

Huntington House Publishers
P.O. Box 53788
Lafayette, Louisiana 70505

Library of Congress Card Catalog Number 95-75428
ISBN 1-56384-089-8

Printed in the U.S.A.

This book is dedicated to Marian, Lenore, David, Jonathan, Katie, Emily, and my law partner, Don Coffman, without whose patience and understanding I could never have completed such a project.

Contents

Introduction

In the 1980s, the state of Arkansas was a hotbed of drug-smuggling and gun-running activity. It was also known for political corruption. In the mid-1980s, Arkansas was rapidly becoming a center for small scale industrial production, as state government-backed, low-interest bonds were readily available through ADFA, the Arkansas Development Finance Authority. Arkansas banks offered some of the lowest revolving-credit interest rates in the country, due in part to changes in state banking laws.

At the helm of the ship of state during those years of radical change stood Gov. Bill Clinton. Clinton had been the youngest person ever elected state attorney general. He was also the youngest governor ever elected. Hillary Rodham Clinton, Arkansas' new First Lady, was a Chicago "yankee," who had been a radical left-wing activist in the early seventies. She had worked in Sen. George McGovern's presidential campaign and, in 1974, as a recent Yale Law School graduate, took part in the Watergate proceedings. Her welcome into the inner circle of Arkansas power brokers was less than warm, but she soon developed a reputation as a competent lawyer, joining the prominent Rose Law Firm during Bill's first term as governor, and later serving on the board of directors of a handful of Arkansas' Fortune 500 companies, including Wal-Mart.

In the 1980s and early 1990s, Bill Clinton's Arkansas was a veritable gold mine for those who were "properly" connected. In Little Rock, the Stephens brothers, Witt and Jackson, owned and controlled the largest investment banking operation west of Wall Street. Jackson Stephens had been Jimmy Carter's roommate at Annapolis, and the two had kept in touch over the years. It was through Carter that Stephens learned of Bert Lance's financial plight and helped facilitate Lance's bailout, ultimately making a way for the Pakistani-run BCCI (the Bank of Credit and Commerce International) to get its foot in the door of the American banking market.

If Arkansas of the 1980s was something of a regional center for banking and small industry, it was an international center for drug-smuggling, gun-running, and money-laundering operations. Mena, a western Arkansas community with a population of about fifty-five hundred, located eight miles from the Oklahoma border, was headquarters for the arms-smuggling and drug-trafficking operations of a notorious soldier of fortune named Barry Seal. At Rich Mountain Aviation, Seal equipped airplanes with illegal navigation devices, cargo doors, fuel system modifications, and even special "plumbing," to make long-distance nonstop flights to and from Central and South America and the Caribbean possible.

Apparently, a number of banks in Fort Smith, Pine Bluff, Mena, and other Arkansas cities and towns weren't overly concerned in the 1980s about federal laws requiring the formal reporting of all cash transfers of ten thousand dollars or more. To people like Little Rock "bond daddy," Dan Lasater, a convicted cocaine dealer and close friend of the Clintons, such nonchalance made laundering drug money as easy as shooting fish in a barrel. As long as cash transfer receipts weren't required, the efforts of federal agencies, such as the DEA (Drug Enforcement Administration), the Federal Bureau of Investigation, and the Internal Revenue Service, to investigate suspected money-laundering schemes were significantly hamstrung.

If you had the right political connections in Bill Clinton's Arkansas, you could practically get away with murder. In fact, the likelihood of any mysterious death being deemed a suicide was extremely high. State Medical Examiner Fahmy Malak, a Clinton appointee who had twice covered for Clinton's mother in medical malpractice and wrongful death cases, made sure of that.

Drug dealers and murderers didn't have too much to worry about while Clinton was in office if they knew the right people. You see, unlike most jurisdictions, Arkansas precluded prosecutors from convening grand juries on their own. By law, they had to have the governor's approval, and Clinton's approval wasn't always obtainable.

Clinton also learned something about the use of force in dealing with clandestine cults while he was governor of Arkansas. In 1985, agents from the FBI and the ATF (Bureau of Alcohol, Tobacco, and Firearms), along with the Arkansas National Guard, were called on by the governor to deal with a situation involving a white supremacist group which called itself the Covenant, the Sword, and the Arm of the Lord. William Buford, who had become the resident agent in charge of the ATF office in Little Rock by the time he took part in the siege of the Branch Davidian compound outside Waco, Texas, helped plan the raid in Arkansas.

Bill Clinton's Arkansas of the 1980s was something of a microcosm of Bill Clinton's America of the 1990s. The parallels are uncanny. As governor, Clinton controlled state financial operations by giving bureaucratic appointments to his cronies and supporters and by insuring that he had the last word in determining who benefited from state-backed bond issues facilitated through ADFA. As president, Clinton appointed close friends, like Roger Altman, to key positions in the Treasury Department and the RTC (Resolution Trust Corporation). In Arkansas, Clinton was able to control felony prosecutions to an extent, by insuring that he had the last word on whether or not a grand jury could be convened. As president, Clinton appointed Janet Reno (a friend of First Lady Hillary Rodham Clinton and her brother Hugh Rodham) as head of the Justice Department, the main branch of the federal government dealing with law enforcement and criminal prosecution. He also appointed close friend, and former law partner of the First Lady, Webb Hubbell, as associate attorney general, the number three position at the Justice Department. As governor, he helped get numerous county prosecutors elected. As president, he has placed his imprimatur on Attorney General Reno's appointments of friends like former campaign worker Paula Casey, as U.S. attorney in cities like Little Rock. Clinton appointed Fahmy Malak as state medical examiner in Arkansas. Malak ruled that certain mysterious deaths, like those of two Saline County teen-agers, were suicides. As president, Clinton approved Attorney General Reno's appointment of Robert Fiske, Jr., to investigate the suicide of close friend and former law partner of the First Lady, Deputy White House Counsel Vincent Foster, Jr. That suicide occurred the day after Clinton fired FBI Director William Sessions. While Clinton was governor, the First Lady made sure certain files related to the Whitewater Development Corporation were shredded by employees of the Rose Law Firm. On the day Vince Foster died, the First Lady's chief assistant, Maggie Williams, joined White House Counsel Bernie Nussbaum and another White House staffer, Patsy Thomasson, in rifling through Foster's files while holding law enforcement agents at bay under the pretext of "executive privilege." Thomasson, chief of administration at the Clinton White House, ran Dan Lasater's bond-brokerage while Lasater was serving time on federal cocaine charges.

These and other similarities between the way the Clintons ran Arkansas and the way they are trying to run America, are too numerous to be written off as mere coincidence and too significant to be considered minor aberrations or anomalies. A number of deaths, beginning in 1986 with Barry Seal's assassination at a Baton Rouge, Louisiana, halfway house, and hopefully ending with the suicides of Kathy Ferguson and her boyfriend in Little Rock in 1994, are all directly or indirectly linked to Bill Clinton. We might well add to these the names of over seventy men, women, and children who were members of David Koresh's militant Branch Davidian cult and who died at the cult's compound in Waco in the spring of 1993.

According to some, like Terry Reed, who claims to have taken part in certain covert operations in and around Mena in the early 1980s, the Nicaraguan Freedom Fighters were being supplied with illegally constructed M-16 rifles, explosives, and other contraband under the direction of former U.S. Marine Lt. Col. Oliver North, who was, at the time, a CIA operative. According to others, like Larry Nichols, who claims to have been a Clinton insider during this time period, the cocaine money laundered in banks affiliated with BCCI, here and abroad, largely through the efforts of Dan Lasater, provided the financial foundation for Bill Clinton's rise to power. Some contend that the cocaine was supplied by the Medellin cartel, a group of ruthless thugs and robber barons from the rain-soaked mountainous region in Colombia of the same name, where the coca plant flourishes. Others point to former Panamanian dictator Gen. Manuel Noreiga.

Regardless of which theory you subscribe to, it cannot be gainsaid that Bill Clinton's Arkansas was open for business to drug traffickers, gun runners, and drug money launderers in a big way. And, if such peccant activities were commonplace, it should come as no surprise that extortion, embezzlement, bank fraud, and even a murder or two may have occurred.

The purpose of this book is neither to condemn Bill Clinton nor to accuse him of plotting anyone's death. However, the Latin legal maxim *res ipsa loquitur* almost seems to apply because of the conspicuous connection between Clinton's political activities and connections, and the deaths of a startling number of people who either possessed personal information, or had the misfortune of having befriended those possessing information, about drug smuggling, gun running, money laundering, and murder in Arkansas in the 1980s.

I encourage you to weigh the evidence, consider the facts, and arrive at your own conclusions. Bill Clinton is either the most gullible and naive individual ever to occupy the Oval Office, or he is a treacherous beast who will stop at nothing to achieve his political goals. We may never know the truth, but we can at least investigate why so many in his circle of power have become part of this circle of death.

Chapter One

A Rose by Any Other Name

To say that the Rose Law Firm is something of an "institution" in the "Land of Opportunity," as Arkansas calls itself, is putting it mildly. The firm was founded in 1820, sixteen years before Arkansas became a state. Its founders were Chester Ashley, who would later become a United States senator, and Robert Crittenden, Arkansas' first territorial secretary.

In 1865, the very powerful lawyer U.M. Rose joined forces with George C. Watkins. Watkins was an early chief justice of the Arkansas Supreme Court and a previous partner of Ashley. It was from this union that the firm got its name. The prominence of U.M. Rose is undeniable. He is one of only two Arkansans whose statues stand in the halls of the United States Capitol. Mr. Rose also has the distinction of having been a founder of the American Bar Association. He served as the ABA's president in 1900.

In addition to men like Rose, Ashley, and Crittenden, six members of the Rose firm have distinguished themselves by serving on the Arkansas Supreme Court. Three of those, including commercial law specialist Webster L.

"Webb" Hubbell, presided as chief justice. Another partner has served as a United States bankruptcy judge, and another as an Arkansas state representative.

Along with Hubbell, three other prominent former members of the Rose firm specialized in commercial and corporate law and securities: C. Joseph Giroir, Jr., Hillary Rodham Clinton, and Vincent W. Foster, Jr. Foster died in July 1993.

Giroir, born in Pine Bluff in 1939, was educated at the University of Arkansas, earning an L.L.B. (bachelor of laws) in 1963. He then attended Georgetown, where he received a master of laws degree (L.L.M.) in taxation in 1965. At the time he joined the Rose firm, Giroir was probably the only lawyer in Arkansas with an L.L.M. in taxation from a well-respected law school. The Stephens companies, the largest investment banking concern outside of Wall Street, knew that and retained Rose in 1977 to handle their corporate affairs.[1]

If Giroir's legal prowess was well-recognized, he was also politically savvy. In the mid-seventies he lobbied the Arkansas legislature on behalf of clients like Stephens, Inc., to legalize the formation of bank holding companies. At the same time, he helped change the usury laws to make commercial banking in Arkansas more attractive.

Applying his knowledge of banking and commercial law to an ever-expanding menu of business opportunities, Giroir was personally able to obtain a controlling interest in four Arkansas banks. He eventually sold his interests to the Stephens-owned Worthen Banking Corporation, a holding company established under the new laws Giroir had lobbied for. Giroir netted $53,760,294 in cash, stocks and other securities, and notes as a result of the Worthen sale.[2]

Worthen later became a major depository for Arkansas state tax receipts, but, in 1985, it lost $52 million of taxpayers' money by purchasing government securities

through a New Jersey brokerage house that had a reputation for churning accounts, speculating, and engaging
in other high-risk practices. Worthen almost went bankrupt, but was bailed out in the nick of time by loans
from its stockholders. Giroir was later charged with securities fraud in a derivative action filed by an angry
Worthen stockholder. As a result, Giroir lost his position as a member of Worthen's board of directors, and
Rose lost Worthen as a client.

Worse yet, Giroir was dragged into court by the
Federal Savings and Loan Insurance Corporation (FSLIC)
because of his ongoing relationship with FirstSouth, a
Pine Bluff savings institution with the dubious distinction of being the first billion-dollar thrift failure in the
country. FirstSouth's CEO went to jail, along with its
lawyer, who happened to be the former president of the
Arkansas Bar Association. Giroir narrowly escaped personal financial ruin in the FSLIC proceeding by filing a
countersuit against the government. Rose was not as
fortunate. Because of Giroir's use of the firm's letter-
head in rendering legal advice beneficial to both
FirstSouth and himself, Rose was ultimately forced to
settle by paying five hundred thousand dollars to the
federal government.[3] Giroir's fall from grace led to his
parting company with Rose. After he left, he formed his
own law firm in Little Rock; Giroir and Gregory.

Like Giroir, Webb Hubbell specialized in commercial law and securities. Hubbell was also a politician. A
football star at the University of Arkansas, the six-foot,
six-inch Hubbell almost had a chance to play in the NFL
for the Chicago Bears. Returning to Little Rock in the
early seventies, Hubbell hired on as an associate with
Rose. He was elected mayor of Little Rock in 1979 and
held that position until 1981. In 1984, he served as chief
justice of the Arkansas Supreme Court.

Much of Hubbell's political success can be attributed
to his wife's family's connections. He married Suzanna

Ward, the oldest daughter of Seth Ward. Seth Ward
owned the Triple S Ranch, just outside of Little Rock.
Ranching, however, was Ward's hobby. He also owned
a company called Park-O-Meter, Inc. (POM), which operated a small manufacturing plant in Russellville, Arkansas. Originally designed for the production of parking meters, POM apparently underwent a radical facelift
in the mid-1980s, while Hubbell was a member of its
board of directors. With a few new milling machines, a
couple of new lathes, and an assortment of expensive
adapters and conversion kits, POM would soon be manufacturing something quite different from parking meters.

Hillary Rodham Clinton was born in Chicago, Illinois, in October 1947. She graduated from Wellesley
College in Massachusetts in 1969. A liberal, she worked
for Sen. George McGovern's presidential campaign
against Richard Nixon in 1972. In 1973, she received her
juris doctor degree from Yale. It was at Yale that she met
Bill Clinton. After a brief stint in 1974 as counsel for the
House Judiciary Committee's Impeachment Inquiry Staff,
which was part of the Watergate investigation, the new
Ms. Rodham Clinton followed her husband back to his
home state of Arkansas.

Both she and Bill taught at the University of Arkan-
sas Law School at Fayetteville in the mid-seventies until
Bill ran for and was elected Arkansas attorney general.
After the election, they moved to Little Rock, and the
university hired her as an associate professor of law at its
Little Rock campus. Finally, in 1977, she left her teach-
ing position and began working as an associate with the
Rose firm.

While at Rose, in addition to the hectic demands of
the day-to-day practice of law in a big (at least by Arkansas standards) firm, Rodham Clinton managed, rather
miraculously, to chair the Children's Defense Fund, the
Legal Services Corporation, and the Commission on
Women in the Profession. She also found time to sit on

the boards of four major corporations in Arkansas: Wal-Mart, TCBY Yogurt, Southern Development Bancorp, and Lafarge (a French-based cement company). Of course, she was handsomely rewarded for her board duties, receiving over sixty-four thousand dollars in fees in 1991 alone, in addition to her regular salary at the law firm.[4] She also represented and worked closely with chicken magnate Donald Tyson.

Vincent W. Foster, Jr., or Vince, as he was known to his friends, was born in January 1945, in Hope, Arkansas. He grew up with Bill Clinton and Clinton's former White House Chief of Staff Thomas E. "Mack" McLarty. In fact, the only photograph anyone recalls being displayed on the wall in Foster's office at the White House was one featuring himself, Clinton, and McLarty in their kindergarten class in Hope.

Foster attended tiny Davidson College, in Davidson, North Carolina, and graduated in 1967. He started law school at Vanderbilt, in Nashville, Tennessee, but finished the course work for his juris doctor degree at the University of Arkansas in 1971. As a rising star of sorts in the clannish Arkansas legal community, Foster was one of a handful of lawyers who knew something about securities and commercial law. Consequently, those were the areas he concentrated on, in ultimately becoming a partner in the Rose Law Firm.

The offices of Foster, Hubbell, and Rodham Clinton were arranged very close to each other in the Rose building, a renovated YMCA in downtown Little Rock. The close proximity of the offices was reflective of the truly close friendship the three lawyers apparently shared. Unlike Rose, trial attorneys who represented insurance companies against accident victims or who appeared in criminal court to defend drug dealers, Foster, Hubbell, and Rodham Clinton had a more refined, silk-stocking clientele. They also had more opportunities than most to get involved in potentially high-return investments like certain real estate limited partnerships and joint ventures, cattle futures, and international banking. One such investment was a real estate joint venture in which Rodham Clinton, her husband Bill, and James and Susan McDougal were partners. It was called the Whitewater Development Corporation.

When Bill Clinton became the forty-second president of the United States in January 1993, he invited Foster, Hubbell and a number of other prominent, and not-so-prominent, Arkansans with him to Washington, D.C. Hubbell was quickly installed as the number three man at the Justice Department, which of course is run by the attorney general of the United States, and controls the U.S. attorney's office in every federal jurisdiction. Foster accepted the position as deputy White House counsel. And, just as she had done when her husband had been elected attorney general of Arkansas, Hillary Rodham Clinton followed him to a new mansion in a new capital city.

Endnotes

1. According to L.J. Davis, writing in *The New Republic* ("The Name of Rose," 4 April 1994), at the time the Stephens concerns hired Rose, Giroir was considered the only true securities law specialist in Arkansas.

2. Davis, *The New Republic.*

3. Ibid.

4. Ibid.

Chapter Two

Deputy White House Counsel Vince Foster

At approximately one o'clock that afternoon on Tuesday, 20 July 1993, Deputy White House Counsel Vince Foster left his office, telling staff members he would see them later. Around six o'clock that evening, two U.S. Park Service employees reported that they had found the body of a man who appeared to be in his late forties on an embankment at Fort Marcy Park. The park is one of several small, and rather obscure, fortifications placed along the Potomac River by order of Abraham Lincoln for the protection of the District of Columbia during the Civil War. Located at McLean, Virginia, near Langley (the home of the Central Intelligence Agency), about three miles from Washington, D.C., Fort Marcy is a public park maintained by the federal park service. The body was soon identified as that of Deputy White House Counsel Vince Foster.

The park service employees who reported that Foster's body was at Fort Marcy did not initially discover it. They say that a heavy-set, middle-aged, white man in a white utility-type van (a panel truck) pulled into the parking lot at the park service facility where they were working, told them there was "a dead body on the embankment in the park," suggested that they telephone the police, and slowly drove off.[1] After advising the emergency operator of the man's report, the two workers went to Fort Marcy Park themselves, but couldn't see the body from the road leading up to the park or from the parking area. When emergency medical personnel arrived, they said they had been told by an unidentified woman that there was "a dead body on the embankment" at Fort Marcy Park.[2]

The foregoing is but one version of the initial series of events that occurred on that hot July evening in 1993. What follows is an analysis of the various renditions offered by the White House staff, park service employees, paramedics, park police, and others since that time.

The Official White House Position

A number of White House press conferences and press releases have dealt with Vince Foster's death. For example, the day after Foster's body was discovered, Bill Clinton said he had no idea why Foster "took his life," clearly implying that in his opinion Foster had committed suicide. White House Communications Director Mark Gearan gave a press conference that same day. When he was specifically asked whether a suicide note had been found, Gearan replied, evasively, that Foster "never said anything to any of his colleagues here in the White House or his friends here in Washington that would indicate that anything was out of the ordinary."

Setting the suicide note issue aside momentarily, and presuming Gearan's sincerity, his response should be read in light of the following, from an article by John Corry in the October 1993 edition of the *American Spectator.*

> *Newsweek* had reported . . . that the same day her husband's body was found in fort Marcy Park, Mrs. [Lisa] Foster had confided to Mack McLarty's wife in the Garden Terrace Restaurant of the Four Seasons Hotel [that] Vince Foster was "having trouble handling the pressure. He couldn't sleep, and he was losing weight. He seemed down. He couldn't let go." But even as Mrs. McLarty tried to cheer up her friend, *Newsweek* said "Vince Foster was driving out of the White House gates in his Honda Accord" on his way to Fort Marcy.[3]

Corry then notes that *Time* magazine contained a different report:

> *Time* said Mrs. Foster and Mrs. McLarty were at the Foster's new house at about the same time Foster "passed through the iron gate of the White House in his gray Nissan." . . . *Time* said authoritatively that Mrs. Foster told Mrs. McLarty "that Vince's distraction—no one called it depression— had lifted during a getaway weekend on Maryland's Eastern Shore."[4]

Vince Foster and Thomas E. "Mack" McLarty were lifelong friends. If Foster was suicidal, it's highly likely his close friends would have noticed symptoms of the type of severe depression that leads a person to take his own life. Of course, that presumption adds credibility to the reports in both *Time* and *Newsweek* that Foster had been "down," was losing weight, and had been "distracted" prior to his death. However, the statement attributed to Mrs. Foster about their "getaway weekend" has a genuine ring of sincerity to it and refutes the notion that Vince Foster, a devoted husband, father of three, and counsel to the president of the United States, was so emotionally distraught and unable to cope with the pressures of his job that he shot himself.

Two days after Foster's body was discovered, White House Press Secretary Dee Dee Myers held a press con-

ference. When asked about a positive identification on
the weapon Foster allegedly used to shoot himself, Myers
advised that the Bureau of Alcohol, Tobacco, and Firearms (ATF) was having trouble because of the age of the
pistol, a .38 caliber Colt revolver believed to have been
manufactured around 1913, and the fact that it didn't
have a serial number. When asked if a search had been
conducted of Foster's office and if anything in the way
of evidence had been found, Myers responded:

> [T]he Park Police were in [Foster's office] this
> morning. They've interviewed a number of staff
> members about Vince's last day, and will be sort
> of, I think, finishing up with their look today
> here in terms of Vince's office. They're simply
> trying to confirm their preliminary notion that it
> was, in fact, a suicide.

Then, when asked to confirm whether members of
the White House Counsel's Office were, because of "the
client relationship with the President," physically involved
in the investigation when the park police went into
Foster's office, Myers responded as follows:

> Yes, I would imagine that there will be somebody
> from the—I don't know exactly how that's—and I
> can certainly get back to you on exactly physically
> how that works. But I think that there will be
> somebody from the Counsel's Office there just to
> help to assist with that. Actually . . . I'm not sure
> how it's going to work.

As a practical matter, however, no one, except perhaps the president and the First Lady, was in a better
position than Myers to be cognizant of the fact that
three White House staff members had, ostensibly by
claiming "executive privilege," intervened in the investigation, physically entered Foster's office for a couple of
hours while holding legitimate law enforcement agents
at bay, and apparently removed a large number of files

to the third floor of the White House for "storage" near the First Family's living quarters.

According to the Congressional Record of 2 August 1994, Chief of Staff Mack McLarty learned of Vince Foster's death shortly after nine o'clock on the evening his body was discovered.[5] McLarty immediately ordered Foster's office sealed. To Clinton insiders, however, "sealed" is apparently not synonymous with "locked" because the door was actually left unlocked all night. In fact, within minutes after the news of Foster's death had been communicated to them, White House Counsel Bernard Nussbaum, First Lady Hillary Rodham Clinton's Chief of Staff Margaret A. "Maggie" Williams, and White House Director of Administration Patsy Thomasson were removing records from Foster's office. The records included the Clintons' tax returns, as well as files containing information about their Whitewater Development Corporation investment. Federal law enforcement authorities weren't advised of this until much later, and the White House didn't confirm it until December 1993.[6]

Nussbaum has said they were in Foster's office for ten minutes, but the park police, who were kept outside while the White House staffers rifled through the files, said they were in Foster's office for over two hours.

Two days later, Nussbaum and other White House officials searched Foster's office again. This time some of the documents culled from his files were sent to Foster's personal attorney, James Hamilton. During this second search, Nussbaum again cited executive privilege, to keep the park police and FBI agents from even watching them sift through the files.

In an effort to protect Nussbaum, Williams, Thomasson, and the others from further scrutiny, White House Press Secretary Dee Dee Myers created the impression that it was the law enforcement agencies, not the White House staffers, who were lying: "Mr. Nussbaum went through and sort of described the contents of each of the files and what was in the drawers while representatives of the Justice Department, the Secret Service, the FBI, and other members of the counsel's office were present."[7] Perhaps what Ms. Myers meant by "present" was that agents from those various law enforcement groups were somewhere in the White House during Nussbaum's fishing expedition. However, other White House sources close to the investigation confirmed that FBI agents and park police had been ordered to sit in chairs in the hallway outside Foster's office, and Secret Service agents weren't even permitted to be in the area while Nussbaum, Williams, and Thomasson went through Foster's files. They also said that Nussbaum gave no indication to either the FBI or the park police of what he was taking. One FBI agent was actually reprimanded when he stood up and peeked into the room in an effort to see what was taking them so long.

It was not until a week after the second search, when park police investigators met with Foster's attorney, James Hamilton, to review Foster's personal diary, that they learned about the removal of the Whitewater records. Hamilton only allowed the investigators to briefly inspect Foster's diary and a few other documents. He absolutely refused to allow them to make photocopies of anything, citing privacy concerns and the attorney-client privilege. Hamilton later refused a request from the Justice Department for access to the diary and other documents.

The Suicide Notes

According to the Congressional Record on 27 July 1993, the White House revealed that on 26 July it had found a suicide note, supposedly written by Foster. It was in the "bottom" of his briefcase, torn into twenty-seven pieces. The note contained no fingerprints, though there was a smudged palm print.[8]

On 29 July, Myers conducted another press conference, in part to deal with this recent evidentiary finding.

She began by referring questions about the note to the Justice Department, but, in the next breath, she discussed its contents, saying that it was "work-related" and that she believed it "sort of shed some light on his state of mind, assuming that [the note] is authenticated." "Beyond that," she added, "we can't really comment given that it is part of an ongoing investigation."

During that press conference, Myers admitted that White House staffers had gone into Foster's office and had done some of their own "investigating." Moreover, her responses contained the rather damning admission that the staff essentially committed one or more federal criminal offenses by failing to immediately turn over evidence (i.e., the note) to the investigating authorities.[9] After admitting the White House had had the note for over twenty-four hours before it was turned over to the park police, she went on to explain her answer:

> It was our judgment that the best thing to do was to make sure that the family had a chance to see [the note]. Lisa [Mrs. Vincent] Foster was coming to Washington on Tuesday for business unrelated to this letter and was given—was informed about it when she got here. And the President, who was out of town on Monday, was also informed on Tuesday.

Myers then advised that after Foster's family was given an opportunity to examine the note, the White House "promptly called the Justice Department," apparently to formally advise the FBI about what had been discovered.

According to the *Washington Times*, documents produced in federal court in Washington, D.C., in the Travelgate proceedings, contain references to Foster's alleged suicide note. That version of the note includes an obvious reference to the scandal then developing in the White House travel office. It also allegedly discusses an adulterous affair between Foster and Hillary Rodham

Clinton.[10] Because the Travelgate note deals with two specific issues which could well have burdened Foster so much that he was driven to the point of desperation, and ultimately suicide, it is the more likely of the two notes allegedly in existence to be authentic.

But, at least two sources outside the White House, the park police and the official investigators, claim to have seen another suicide note. The following is the reconstructed text:

> I value my integrity, I worked hard to become an outstanding lawyer. The Clinton Whitehouse [*sic*] was an entirely new environment for me. Major players in the Clinton Whitehouse [*sic*] seem to think they can cover-up realities with words and slogans, but I think I can honestly say, as Nixon did in 1973 at Disneyland, "I am not a crook."

> The fact is, I am not a crook. Your wife is a crook. I suppose I could go back to the law firm in Little Rock. God, I wish I'd never left it, but now I can't. I know too much about the Clinton Whitehouse [*sic*].

> I really don't want to hurt you, Bill. I remember those days in Little Rock. If I have to testify there would be impeachment proceedings, obstruction of Justice, abuse of power, crimes and misdea-menours [*sic*], the old Constitutional language.

> Your wife is a lawyer. Why didn't she know better? I can't dodge the issue. I also can't bear the prospect of testifying against you and Mrs. Clinton.

> Bill, you think you can sell anything with hon-eyed words, but words do not connect with real-ity. It's disaster time Bill. I have an old fashioned revolver. There is a tiny park overlooking the Potomac River. It has a Civil War cannon. We have come to the parting of the ways. Good luck partner.

> /s/ Vince[11]

In reviewing this alleged suicide note, a number of questions arise which render its authenticity extremely dubious. First, keeping in mind that lawyers are men of words, one would think a man of Foster's education, training, and background would refer to the president's official residence and the location of his office, as the "White House," not the "Whitehouse." A lawyer of Vince Foster's stature would likely be inclined, out of habit if for no other reason, to be very accurate in his choice and use of words. For that reason, it would also be incongruous for Foster to use vulgar terms like "major players" in referring to high-ranking White House staffers.

The passing reference to Richard Nixon's denial of dishonesty, which he made at Disneyland in 1973, is almost laughable. If it was designed to lead the reader to believe Foster was trying to leave a subtle clue about the potential for scandal in the Clinton White House by harking back to Watergate, it falls miserably short.

The third paragraph of the alleged Foster suicide note really strains credulity. To begin with, of all people, lawyers know that the Fifth Amendment to the United States Constitution, which is applicable in any legal, equitable, or administrative proceeding, regardless of venue, permits a witness to refuse to answer any question posed to him while he's under oath. To that must be added the rather ironclad protection of the attorney-client privilege. If Vince Foster actually believed he would be required to testify against Bill Clinton, then temporary amnesia should be added to the list of conditions he was suffering from when he wrote the alleged suicide note.

Another phrase in the third paragraph, and which also makes the note extremely suspect, is the maladroit reference to "crimes and misdeamenours [*sic*], the old Constitutional language." No medical examiner worth his salt should fail to order a complete analysis of body fluids to check for traces of narcotic drugs or alcohol upon learning that such butchery of the English language had been engaged in by the deputy White House counsel.

The fifth paragraph is suspect, if for no other reason than attributing to Foster—a lifelong friend of the president and former law partner of the First Lady—the use of the very formal title Mrs. Clinton in referring to Hillary Rodham Clinton. A feminist, Rodham Clinton is known to have shunned the use of the Clinton surname for several years after their marriage. Surely Foster, a close friend and law partner, would've referred to Rodham Clinton either by her first name or in some other less formal manner.

The first sentence of the sixth, and final paragraph of the alleged Foster suicide note is one of the few having a ring of truth to it. Objectively speaking, even the casual observer must realize that Bill Clinton, like a lot of other politicians, probably thinks he can "sell anything with honeyed words." Foster definitely could have made that statement. But, the wording of the rest of the paragraph is a little more problematic. For example, it is difficult to imagine why Foster, or anyone else with a wife and children, would've gone into detail in a suicide note about the weapon he planned to use and the location he chose for his death, while neglecting to even mention, much less say goodbye to, his family. On the contrary, the mention of a "tiny park overlooking the Potomac River" and a "Civil War cannon" seem rather to confirm the notion that the note was designed to create the illusion that Foster took his own life with an old .38 caliber pistol, near a Civil War cannon at Fort Marcy Park, Virginia.

The alleged suicide note was found by Associate White House Counsel Steve Neuwirth at the "bottom of Vince's briefcase" which was in Foster's office. According to the White House, Neuwirth found the note, torn into twenty-seven pieces, as he was packing up some of Foster's personal belongings, which were to be turned over to the family.

On 30 July 1993, Press Secretary Dee Dee Myers blamed the tardiness with which the note was found on the ineptness of the park police, telling reporters that while the briefcase had been in Foster's office when park police detectives had searched there for evidence, they simply failed to discover it. A more believable conclusion is that the note didn't exist when the park police conducted their search.

Unanswered questions about Foster's briefcase continued into January 1995, when Travelgate prosecutors subpoenaed three of the emergency medical technicians who arrived at Fort Marcy shortly after the body was discovered. The men had observed the briefcase on the seat of Foster's car.

Again, during her 30 July press conference, Myers insisted that the file-fishing expeditions conducted by White House staffers in Foster's office, both on the evening his body was discovered and over the next couple of days, were done under the watchful eye of "representatives of the Justice Department, the Secret Service, the FBI and other members of the Counsel's Office." Those same law enforcement authorities have repeatedly denied being allowed to do anything but sit on chairs in the hallway outside Foster's office, while Nussbaum, Williams, Thomasson, and others rifled through the evidence, hiding under the protective veil of "executive privilege."

The Fiske Report

If the authenticity of the alleged suicide note is questionable, the account of the circumstances surrounding Foster's death, as reported by Robert B. Fiske, Jr., is simply unbelievable.

Fiske, a partner in the prominent New York City law firm of Davis, Polk, and Wardwell, and a well-connected Democrat, was educated at Yale and the University of Michigan. Between 1976 and 1980, he was the U.S. attorney for the southern district of New York (New York City). Fiske was appointed by U.S. Attorney General Janet Reno as the special investigator to study and report on the possible connections between Whitewater Development Corporation, the collapse of Madison Guaranty Savings & Loan Association, and the death of Vince Foster. After four-and-a-half months and two federal grand jury investigations (in which no indictments were returned), Fiske released his report, entitled "Report of the Independent Counsel in re Vince Foster, Jr.," on 30 June 1994, less than a year after the alleged suicide occurred.

Ninety-one pages of Fiske's almost two hundred-page report contain resumes and curriculum vitae of the forensic pathologists and other medical experts who nonrestrictively endorsed Virginia pathologist James Beyer's autopsy report. Incredibly, however, Dr. Beyer's own resume is not contained in the report. The portion dealing with Foster's alleged suicide comprises only fifty-eight pages.[12]

Beyer, who at the time the Fiske report was completed was seventy-six years old, has a rather weak track record as a medical examiner. For example, in 1989, after Beyer officially deemed the death of twenty-one-year-old Timothy Easley a suicide, the young man's girlfriend, Candy Wharton, came forward and confessed to the killing. Relatives had noticed a cut on the victim's hand, which Dr. Harry Bonnell, chief medical examiner of San Diego, California, later said was a classic defense wound. Beyer had apparently noticed the cut but wrote it off as being "consistent with a needle mark" and failed to include any reference to it at all in the autopsy report.[13]

In another supposed suicide, it was later determined that the deceased, Thomas Burkett, Jr., had been attacked and bludgeoned with a blunt object. The family of Burkett, also twenty-one, had noticed a disfigured ear, which he hadn't had in life and which wasn't noted in the autopsy report. The body was exhumed. Another pathologist, Dr. Erik Mitchell, examined Burkett's body and found that his lower jaw had been fractured. This evidence, at the very least, meant that the man might have been beaten shortly before his death. A second autopsy revealed that Beyer had not dissected the lung, as he had indicated in the initial autopsy report.[14]

Sgt. George Gonzalez, a paramedic with Fairfax County Fire & Rescue Station No. 1, received a call shortly before 6:00 P.M. on 20 July 1993, advising that a rescue unit was needed at Fort Marcy Park to check on an apparent shooting victim. In his original rendition of what happened next, Gonzalez related that when the paramedics arrived at the park, shortly after 6:00 P.M., they split into two teams, one of which, led by Gonzalez, went in a northeasterly direction up the main trail to the park. The other team headed south, away from the park.[15]

Fort Marcy Park is a very small, rectangular area of land. It is about twenty feet higher than the land surrounding it. Two Civil War era cannon are located at strategic positions on the edge of the raised slope area, known as the berm. The first cannon, which is closest to the parking area, is near the southern end of the berm on the west side of the park, and sits atop that berm facing northwest. The second cannon is located at the far end of the park on the northernmost berm facing northeast.[16]

In January 1994, Sergeant Gonzalez was interviewed by Christopher Ruddy, a reporter for the *New York Post*. At that time, according to Ruddy, Gonzalez told him that he had approached the first cannon, moved past it, and found nothing. Then, continuing to move in a northerly direction, Gonzalez noticed a body about twenty feet down the berm past the cannon. Gonzalez then shouted for his teammates, who were still in sight, to come and assist him. Moving quickly down the berm to the body, Gonzalez checked the man's vital signs and determined that he was dead. Dr. Donald Haut, the medical examiner whose deputy actually performed the autopsy on Foster's body, went to Fort Marcy Park the night Foster's body was found. His overall impressions, and his description of the park and the location of the body, are basically the same as those initially related by Gonzalez to Ruddy.[17]

The Fiske report contains a much different version of what Gonzalez's rescue team found, and where it found it. First, the report places Foster's body on the berm ten feet in front of the second (northernmost) cannon. Second, Fiske says it was officer Kevin Fornshill of the park police, not Sergeant Gonzalez, who first discovered the body. Fiske has Gonzalez as the third man to arrive there, behind Fornshill and rescue-team paramedic, Todd Hall. Third, it was Hall, not Gonzalez, who checked Foster's vital signs, according to the report. Ruddy reports that Gonzalez has now changed his story and basically agrees with Fiske's rendition, except that he denies seeing Hall or anyone else check Foster's pulse. Gonzalez now says everyone assumed Foster was dead.[18]

Ruddy claims Gonzalez drew a map for him during their January 1994 interview, reflecting where the parking area and walking trails were, where the cannon were located, where Foster's body was found, and where the main thoroughfares, the George Washington Memorial Parkway and the Chain Bridge Road, were located relative to the park.

One piece of evidence that lends credibility to Ruddy's rendition of Gonzalez's original story is the unrehearsed statement by paramedic Kory Ashford, to the effect that he didn't recall seeing a cannon when he went to put Foster's body in the plastic body bag. It had been a clear day, and he'd arrived between 8:30 and 9:00 P.M., which is well before nightfall that time of year in Washington. Had Ashford gone to the second (northernmost) cannon, where the Fiske report placed Foster's body, he could not have missed seeing the cannon because he would have had to walk around it to reach a body lying on the berm just ten feet beyond. Ruddy also reports that an anonymous park police officer confirmed Gonzalez's original story by placing Foster's body at least twenty—and as much as fifty—feet past the first (westernmost) cannon, with his feet pointed west toward the George Washington Parkway.[19]

Another problem with the Fiske report is that the only photographs taken of Foster's body which weren't underexposed clearly show that the body was resting in thick, leaf-covered grass. While the berm near the first cannon (where Gonzalez originally placed the body) contained such vegetation, the berm in front of the second cannon (the official location of Foster's body) was almost bare at the time of Foster's death. The single photograph allegedly leaked to the public and shown on "ABC News" is a snapshot of a man's right hand grasping a pistol in a very awkward manner. Both the park police and the Fiske report maintain that the photo is Foster's hand, yet those who knew him say he was left-handed.[20]

Law enforcement experts maintain that those who commit suicide with handguns generally use the dominant hand. The reason for that is rather obvious. Suicide victims intend to kill themselves. They don't set out to inflict serious but non-fatal injuries. A left-hand-dominant person wouldn't be as likely to do a thorough job using his right hand.

According to Ruddy, John Hanchette, a reporter for *Gannett Newspapers*, was at Fort Marcy Park with a colleague the day after Foster's body was discovered. Hanchette described the work done by park police investigators at the crime scene as "sloppy" and claims to have personally found bloodstains in the dirt in front of the second cannon. Because that location didn't compare well with the alleged photograph of Foster's hand (the ground is relatively bare near the second cannon, yet the photo shows thick vegetation), Hanchette questioned the authenticity of the picture. However, another rescue team member, Lt. Bill Bianchi, who apparently watched as paramedic Kory Ashford placed Foster's body in the body bag, has said that he saw blood on the grass. Again, there was little or no grass in front of the first cannon.[21]

Yet a third location for Foster's body has been reported, this time by the park police. They say the body was found some twenty feet west of the second cannon.[22] But, if the park police are correct, Ashford's unrehearsed claim that he failed to notice a cannon while walking en route to Foster's body is, likewise, of dubious veracity.

Statement of the "Confidential Witness"

On Tuesday, 2 August 1994, in the U.S. House of Representatives, Congressman Dan Burton (R-Ind.) read into the record pertinent portions of a fifty-page affidavit signed by a man whose identity at the time was known only to Burton, two FBI agents, and former Watergate co-conspirator, G. Gordon Liddy.[23] The man is known publicly as the "confidential witness" (CW). What follows are excerpts from Congressman Burton's statement and comparisons between CW's personal testimony, the Fiske report, and statements attributed to paramedic Sgt. George Gonzalez by Christopher Ruddy.

As CW tells it, between 5:30 and 6:00 P.M., on the afternoon of Tuesday, 20 July 1993, he was driving his utility van on the George Washington Memorial Parkway near Fort Marcy Park. He claims he pulled into the park to urinate. There are no restrooms at Fort Marcy, so he walked into the trees in the direction of the second (northernmost) cannon. As he stood there, he glanced around and saw a man lying on the sloping berm a few feet away. He approached to within two or three feet of the man's head and leaned over, looking directly into his face, about sixteen inches above the ground. CW spent between one and two minutes staring at the body. He has consistently maintained that, when he found the body, the man's "head was looking straight up" and "his hands were at his sides, palms up with no gun in either hand."[24] The man was later identified as Deputy White House Counsel Vincent Foster.

The Fiske report quotes CW as saying that he "may have been mistaken"; that "there may have been a gun in Foster's hand"; and that he couldn't see very well "because of the dense foliage and the position of the hand." However, CW contends that FBI agents "pressed" him on the gun issue, asking him "as many as 20 to 25 times" if he "was sure there was no gun." The colloquy went essentially as follows:

> The FBI said, "what if the trigger guard was around the thumb and the thumb was obscured by foliage and the rest of the gun was obscured by the foliage and the hand?" In other words, the trigger guard would be around the thumb, the gun would be underneath the thumb, and a leaf would be over that and you would not see it.
>
> [CW], after being asked about 20 to 25 times, said, "If what you describe were the case, then I suppose it could be possible because I did not count his fingers, but I am sure that the palms were definitely opened and facing up."[25]

At this time, CW still hadn't seen the photograph of what is alleged to be Foster's hand. The photo had somehow left the possession of the park police and had found its way into the hands of "ABC News." In the picture, the right hand is palm down, with the thumb trapped in the trigger guard in a very awkward position. Congressman Burton obtained a copy of the picture and showed it to CW. CW was incredulous. "This is not the way it was" he said. "That hand was moved!"[26]

The Fiske report noted blood on the right side of Foster's face, running down his cheek to his right shoulder, which was also stained with blood. The blood on the shoulder was what is commonly referred to as a "contact stain," indicating that Foster's chin or jaw had, at some point after the blood began trickling down his cheek, come in contact with his right shoulder. Thus, Foster's head was turned to the right some time after he was shot. Fiske did mention that these blood stains were inconsistent with Foster's head being upright but made no mention of possible movement of the body before it was discovered by CW. CW and others believe the stains prove that Foster's head was moved at a time when the blood was still trickling out of his mouth.[27]

Another inconsistent, if not bizarre finding by Fiske, is that Foster's head must have been moved by someone after CW found the body. CW has sworn that Foster's head was facing straight up when he found the body, yet blood had obviously run down the right side of his face, clearly indicating that his head had been turned or had leaned toward the right at some time prior to CW's discovery. Fiske utterly fails to deal with that conundrum and instead simply surmises that "one of the persons who arrived after [CW] moved [Foster's] head," causing the blood to trickle down the right side of his face, onto his shoulder.[28] But, it seems clear that Foster's head had to have been moved to the right sometime before it came to rest looking straight up; otherwise the blood flow defied gravity.

Of course, the obvious answer, assuming the veracity of CW's testimony that he didn't tamper with the body, is that someone moved Foster's head before CW discovered the body. In any event, that's what CW believes and has sworn to. That contention also finds support in the otherwise conflicting accounts of Sergeant Gonzalez, the park police, and Fiske, with respect to the location of Foster's body in the park. In other words, Foster's body was moved at least twice; once after being shot and before CW found it, and again after CW found it and before it was photographed.

A few minutes later, CW got back in his van and drove up the parkway approximately two and a half miles to a park service maintenance facility. By that time, it was nearly 6:00 P.M. CW looked in vain for a telephone and then noticed a couple of workers standing outside. CW motioned to the workers, and the younger of the two walked over to the van. CW asked him if he could use a telephone because he had an emergency. The worker seemed reluctant to help, at least until he assured himself of the exigencies of CW's situation. Impatient, CW finally said, "Fine, are you familiar with Fort Marcy?" "Oh, yeah, I know it well," was the young man's response. "Do you know where the cannons are?" CW queried. The worker replied that he did. "Do you know the one up on the hill to the right? . . . Not the one on the left up there, the one on the right all the way up on top." "Oh, yeah, I know it well," came the confident reply. "Right beside it, down over the bank is a dead man. You call the police and tell them."[29] At approximately 6:00 P.M., park worker Francis Swan called 911 and reported what CW had told him. The emergency operator immediately contacted Fairfax County Fire & Rescue Station No. 1. Sergeant Gonzalez's team was dispatched and arrived at Fort Marcy at approximately 6:09 P.M.

Additional Evidence

Although the FBI and park police investigators searched the park for the bullet that killed Foster, and for skull fragments, the same evening Foster's body was discovered, none were found. Eight-and-a-half months later, on 4 April 1994, sixteen FBI agents and experts again searched Fort Marcy. This time twelve bullets were found, but none matched the .38 caliber Colt revolver allegedly found in Foster's hand. Congressman Burton contacted a California ballistics expert who advised that after passing through a man's skull, a .38 caliber bullet fired from a pistol should travel no more than three hundred to five hundred yards. That means that if Foster did in fact shoot himself at Fort Marcy, the bullet should still have been somewhere in the park.[30]

In addition to failing to find the spent round that killed Vince Foster, no fingerprints were found on the Colt revolver retrieved from the scene. Likewise, there were no fingerprints on any of the twenty-seven pieces of the suicide note found by one of Foster's associates several days after his death.

The FBI's explanation of the absence of latent prints on the weapon was that the heat had probably destroyed them.[31] It must be recalled, however, that Foster was last seen alive by coworkers just after lunch, and his body was removed from the park, along with most of the other readily available physical evidence, before 9:00 P.M. Further, it would have taken him at least an hour to drive to the park from the White House at that time of day. So, in order for the weapon to be exposed to sufficient heat to destroy fingerprints, it would have to have been in direct sunlight for more than a couple of hours. Yet, the area in which Foster's body was found is covered with a canopy of trees, rarely permitting direct sunlight to penetrate all the way to the ground.

Another problem for Fiske is the absence of dirt on Foster's shoes. The FBI crime lab didn't report any "coherent soil" on either Foster's shoes or clothing. According to the Fiske report, the weather was dry the day of Foster's death. In fact, it hadn't rained significantly for nearly a month. Surprised at the FBI's report that only small traces of the mineral compound mica were found on Foster's shoes and clothing, Congressman Burton personally went to the park, on a dry day, and walked from the parking lot to the second cannon. To his surprise, he found that he had dust all over his shoes.[32]

It follows that either Foster removed his shoes and socks, carrying them in his hands as he walked through the park to the site of his suicide, or that he died at some other location, where his feet had only touched pavement, and his body was then carried to Fort Marcy and laid on the berm near the cannon.

While the law enforcement agencies failed to find the spent round that killed Foster, fingerprints on the weapon and suicide note, or dust on his clothes and shoes, they did find blond and light brown hair on Foster's tee shirt, pants, belt, socks, and shoes; carpet fibers of various colors on his jacket, tie, shirt, shorts, pants, belt, socks, and shoes; and semen in his shorts. All the same, none of this, according to Fiske, "provides any evidence of circumstances connected to [Foster's] death."[33]

Perhaps more incredible is the fact that the combined opinion of the four forensic experts who contributed to the report on Foster's death, almost without exception based their conclusions on Dr. Beyer's report. Not one of them actually examined Foster's body.

The Fiske report also states that Beyer was "unable to take x-rays of Mr. Foster's head because his x-ray machine was broken." However, Beyer told the park police that x-rays of Foster's head showed no evidence of bullet fragments in his skull. According to Congressman Burton's ballistics expert, determining if there are bullet fragments in the skull is a key to discerning how far the bullet would've traveled.[34]

The Saudi Arabian ambassador's residence is just across Chain Bridge Road from the park, approximately one hundred yards, as the crow flies, from where the Fiske report placed Foster's body. Also nearby was the mansion of Prince Bandar bin Sultan of Saudi Arabia. Foster's death probably occurred sometime between 2:00

and 5:00 P.M. The ambassador's residence is protected twenty-four hours a day by five trained security guards, three of whom routinely roam the property and periodically check Fort Marcy Park. No one heard a gunshot on the afternoon Foster allegedly shot himself at Fort Marcy. Fiske attributed the failure of anyone to hear the shot to the presence of traffic on Chain Bridge Road, and to the fact that Foster had placed the gun in his mouth, significantly muffling the sound. Congressman Burton had a homicide detective recreate the shooting with an object of the same basic density as a human head. The shot could clearly be heard one hundred yards away, even with an earthmover running in the background.[35]

According to the Fiske report, the postmortem findings in Foster's case "are typical and characteristic of such findings in deaths due to intentional, self-inflicted intra-oral gunshot wounds."[36] Typical? Several experts, along with Sergeant Gonzalez, head of the paramedic team that discovered the body, have said they have never seen such a small amount of blood in a case involving a gunshot wound to the head. Kory Ashford, the paramedic who placed Foster's body in the body bag, didn't even bother to use rubber gloves, there was so little blood. The forensic pathologists' joint explanation echoed Dr. Beyer's far-fetched *ratio decidendi* that the bullet entered the back of Foster's mouth and passed through his brain stem, instantaneously causing his heart to stop pumping blood. However, it is extremely uncommon for the heart to stop immediately under those circumstances because it's on an independent system. It might be expected to continue pumping blood for as long as two minutes after the severance of the brain stem, which would have resulted in a substantial flow of blood from the entry wound in the mouth, as well as from the exit wound.[37]

Another problem with the Fiske report is its nonrestrictive adoption of Beyer's ostensibly oxymoronic finding that the bullet exited the upper rear of Foster's head. Even if Foster had been in an extremely unnatural and awkward position, with his head tilted backward as far as it could go and with the barrel of the pistol jammed inside and pointing toward the rear of the roof of his mouth, unless he had a very weird morphology (with a much higher than normal brain stem), the bullet would have exited through the back of his neck, or possibly the lower rear portion of his skull. Bullets sometimes do strange things when they enter human bodies, but this one wasn't fired from a hunting rifle with lands and grooves in the barrel to augment rotational velocity; it was supposedly fired from a 1913-vintage, .38 caliber Colt revolver. At least one person, Arkansas lawyer Joe Purvis, a lifelong friend of Foster, who viewed the body at Reubel's Funeral Home in Little Rock, was allegedly told by a Reubel employee that there was a small wound in the back of Foster's mouth and another small exit wound in the back of his neck. No wound in the upper back of Foster's head was noticed.[38]

In addition to these inconsistencies, the following should be considered. There was a relative paucity of gunpowder residue in Foster's mouth and none of his teeth were broken, yet he supposedly shot himself at the closest range possible. There were bloodstains on the temporal area above Foster's right ear, yet his body was found lying almost perfectly supine. Park Police Maj. Robert Hines reported that a beeper was on the seat of Foster's car, with a White House number in its memory, yet Fiske says the beeper was on Foster's body, turned off, and there were no numbers in its memory.

There are several other bits of evidence Fiske either ignored, or rejected as not being relevant to the task at hand, because he and his investigation team utterly failed to deal with them. One is the existence of a wine cooler bottle which, according to CW, was located about "24 to 30 inches to the right, between [Foster's] shoulder and elbow, lying on the berm but on the down side of the hill" with "probably one quarter of its contents in the bottle."[39] Interestingly, CW noticed a light purple-colored stain on Foster's right shoulder. When asked if it was blood, he replied, "No, it was very light purple, almost identical to the color of the wine cooler." CW went on to explain: "I do not think it was blood. . . . It looked like he had thrown up on his right shoulder. In the very center there was one small speck area, probably no larger than a silver dollar that was black, that could have been blood in the very center of it."[40]

As CW left the park that afternoon, he also noticed a couple of cars in the parking lot. One was a white Honda. CW noticed that a coat, similar in color to the suit pants the dead man had been wearing, was folded on the passenger's seat. He also noticed a four-pack of wine coolers with two bottles missing on the floor of the car on the passenger's side. The wine coolers were the same brand and color as the one he had seen in the park near the body. The FBI rejected CW's testimony, officially reporting that the white Honda was not Foster's car. No mention of the wine coolers was made in their report. However, nearly nine months later, at the request of the FBI, CW returned to the park with FBI agents, to retrace his steps and regurgitate his story. During that visit, "one of the agents spent about 15 minutes kicking around all of the leaves and everything, looking for the wine cooler bottle."[41] Naturally, CW wondered why they had waited so long to further investigate that seemingly important bit of information.

The FBI reported traces of valium and an antidepressant in Foster's blood. Such drugs, mixed with alcohol, can be a lethal combination. Beyer, on the other hand, reported no trace of drugs of any kind.[42] Could Vince Foster have been dead before he was shot? Some sources say that was the case. At least one writer has suggested that Foster was given a lethal injection of sodium mono-fluoride 10-80 at his office and was later shot, to create the impression he'd committed suicide. [43]

Finally, CW told Congressman Burton and Dana Rohrabacher, a Republican representing California's forty-fifth congressional district, that there was a cabin about five hundred feet from where Foster's body was found. A path from the cabin leads directly to the site, and a private road leading to the cabin from another direction could easily be traveled unnoticed. The FBI apparently didn't even know about the cabin because they were surprised when CW pointed it out to them. CW also told the FBI that when he found the body, the grass and weeds were trampled down in only two areas: where the body was found and back through the trees and brush to the path leading to the cabin. This, however, was apparently not important enough to the FBI to even be mentioned in their report.[44]

Vince Foster was the highest ranking U.S. government official since John F. Kennedy to die in office under what are, at best, questionable circumstances, and the highest ranking government official to commit suicide since James Forrestal, then Secretary of the Navy, did so in 1949. With so many inconsistencies and unanswered questions, too many presumptions are required in order for the official report of Robert Fiske, Jr., to be given the credibility and recognition it seeks. The conclusion that Deputy White House Counsel Vince Foster took his own life at Fort Marcy Park on 20 July 1993 simply cannot be drawn from a careful study of the Fiske report.

Endnotes

1. Christopher Ruddy, *New York Post*, 1 February 1994.

2. Ibid.

3. John Corry, "Killing the Foster Story," *American Spectator*, October 1993.

4. Ibid.

5. Congressional Record, vol. 140, no. 104, House of Representatives, Tuesday, 2 August 1994.

6. Ibid.

7. Ibid.

8. Ibid.

9. 18 U.S.C. Section 1001, makes it a crime, punishable by up to five years in prison, and up to ten thousand dollars in fines, to "conceal material facts in connection with matters within the jurisdiction of a United States Agency." 18 U.S.C. Sections 1503 and 1505, prohibit the obstruction of justice and obstruction of Justice Department or Congressional inquiries. Convicted offenders can be sentenced to a maximum of ten years, and fined up to ten thousand dollars. And, 18 U.S.C. Section 372, prohibits conspiring to prevent any person (including federal agencies) from discharging the duties of office.

10. Paul Bedard, *Washington Times*, 19 December 1994.

11. Matthew Chin, chairman of the American Conservative Media Network, read this note on a nationwide radio talk show on 6 April 1994.

12. Christopher Ruddy, "A Special Report on the Fiske Investigation of the Death of Vincent W. Foster, Jr.," 18 July 1994. Mr. Ruddy is a reporter for the *New York Post*.

13. Congressional Record, vol. 140, no. 104, House of Representatives, Tuesday, 2 August 1994.

14. Ibid.

15. Ruddy, "A Special Report."

16. Ibid.

17. Ibid.

18. Ibid.

19. Ibid.

20. Ibid.

21. Ibid.

22. Ibid.

23. Liddy is also the host of a daily radio talk show, "Radio Free D.C." The confidential witness has been interviewed by Liddy.

24. Congressional Record, vol. 140, no. 104, House of Representatives, Tuesday, 2 August 1994.

25. Ibid.

26. Ibid.

27. Ibid.

28. Ibid.

29. Ibid.

30. Ibid.

31. Ibid.

32. Ibid.

33. Ibid.

34. Ibid.

35. Ibid.

36. Ruddy, "A Special Report."

37. Ibid.

38. Patrick Matrisciana, *The Clinton Chronicles Book* (Hemet, CA: Jeremiah Books, 1994), 129.

39. Congressional Record, vol. 140, no. 104, House of Representatives, Tuesday, 2 August 1994.

40. Ibid.

41. Ibid.

42. Ibid.

43. Matrisciana, *Clinton Chronicles*, 183.

44. Congressional Record, vol. 140, no. 104, House of Representatives, Tuesday, 2 August 1994.

Chapter Three

A Changing of the Guard

Prior to being named Bill Clinton's White House counsel, Bernard W. "Bernie" Nussbaum was a senior partner in the New York law firm of Wachtell, Lipton, Rosen, and Katz. Nussbaum was educated at Columbia and Harvard, where he obtained his law degree, an L.L.B., in 1961. He was assistant U.S. attorney for the southern district of New York from 1962 to 1966. Nussbaum met and worked with Hillary Rodham Clinton, then a recent Yale law graduate, in 1974 when he was senior associate special counsel to the House Judiciary Committee Impeachment Inquiry during the Watergate proceedings.

Nussbaum and Robert Fiske, also a partner in a high-powered New York law firm, are old friends. Like Nussbaum, Fiske too served in the U.S. attorney's office in the southern district of New York. Fiske was actually the U.S. attorney in that district from 1976 to 1980.

When Bill Clinton, in an unprecedented move, fired former federal judge and Reagan-appointee William Sessions as director of the FBI, the day before Vince Foster died, he already had Sessions' replacement in mind.[1] Louis Freeh, a federal judge from Manhattan, had been recommended to Clinton by none other than Fiske. Clinton formally appointed Freeh to the position of FBI director the day after Vince Foster died. Thus, Clinton, Reno, and everyone else involved knew the day Foster died that whatever role the FBI was to play in the investigation of Foster's death would be determined by Freeh, not Sessions.

Ironically, among the several tasks Attorney General Reno assigned to Robert Fiske when he was hired as special counsel to investigate Foster's death, was to find out why the FBI was prohibited from conducting more than a preliminary inquiry into the cause of Foster's death and why the formal investigation was exclusively turned over to the U.S. Park Police. That particular assignment was clearly a subterfuge. Even though Fiske later admitted the FBI had jurisdiction over the case, in tautological fashion he decided the bureau's involvement ended when its preliminary inquiry failed to find indicia of criminal activity.[2]

Sessions presented a somewhat different story, albeit in a very diplomatic fashion. After his firing, he charged that the FBI had been excluded from the Foster investigation because of a "power struggle between the FBI and the Department of Justice," which occurred around the time he was fired. In Sessions' opinion, "the decision about the investigative role of the FBI . . . was therefore compromised."[3] What Sessions was actually saying, in a tactful and unobtrusive way, and without casting aspersions on Clinton's top federal prosecutor, was that he and Reno were in complete disagreement about the bureau's involvement in the Foster case. He may have also meant that under the circumstances the integrity of any FBI investigation might be suspect.

That there was no love lost between Sessions and his boss, Janet Reno, cannot be gainsaid. The Justice Department had been severely criticized for its role at Mt. Carmel, the Branch Davidian compound in Waco, Texas, which was burned to the ground in April 1993 while under siege by the FBI. Apparently, over Sessions' objections, Reno had given the order to storm the compound with Abrams M1-A1 tanks using CS (tear) gas. The ultimate result was the deaths of over seventy men, women, and children.[4]

At any rate, Sessions would no longer be a thorn in Reno's flesh. The Clinton administration now had a company man on its team in the form of Judge Freeh. And, like all other criminal investigations, the extent of the FBI's involvement in the Foster case would be determined by Freeh and Reno.

Between 8:45 and 9:00 P.M., on the evening of 20 July 1994, Vince Foster's body was quietly placed on a gurney by Fairfax County paramedic Kory Ashford and loaded into an ambulance. Fifteen minutes later, White House Chief of Staff Mack McLarty ordered Foster's office sealed. Despite this order, three White House staffers, Bernie Nussbaum, Margaret Williams, and Patsy Thomasson, entered Foster's office and began rifling through his files, removing records. Some of the documents taken from Foster's office by White House staffers were turned over to Bill Clinton's personal attorney, Robert Barnett. Others were given to Foster's lawyer, James Hamilton. Still others contained records concerning a real estate joint venture involving the Clintons, and James and Susan McDougal, known as Whitewater Development Corporation.[5]

In early August 1994, Margaret Williams made the news in connection with her role in the rifling of Foster's files. According to the Congressional Record of 2 August 1994:

> A Whitewater [Development Corporation] file taken from the office of White House Deputy Vince Foster after his death last year was given to Hillary Rodham Clinton's chief of staff and, at the First Lady's direction, transferred to the White House residence before being turned over to

Clinton's personal lawyer. It was unclear yesterday why then-White House Counsel Bernard Nussbaum gave the file to the First Lady's chief of staff, Margaret Williams, rather than transferring it directly to Robert Barnett, the Clintons' personal lawyer at the time.

According to the Congressional Record, Jeremy Hedges, a part-time courier at the Rose Law Firm in Little Rock, told a grand jury he was instructed to shred documents from Vince Foster's files after Robert Fiske announced he was going to look into Whitewater. In February 1994, after Fiske served document subpoenas on certain Rose employees, Hedges and the other couriers employed at Rose were summoned to a meeting with Rose partners Ronald Clark and Jerry Jones. During the meeting, Jones challenged Hedges' recollection that the documents he had shredded were Foster's. Jones cautioned Hedges not to make faulty assumptions and not to relate assumptions to any investigators. Hedges retorted that he hadn't assumed anything. He related that all the folders in the boxes he had been instructed to destroy were marked "VWF," which are Foster's initials. They were marked in the same way Rose marked all files at the time, with the attorney's initials on the folder. Jones then cautioned Hedges about assuming that any files which might have been Foster's contained information about Whitewater. Hedges could only respond that he had no idea what was in the files because they were shredded so fast. But, another Rose employee had specifically been instructed to shred documents relating to the Clintons' involvement in Whitewater, on 3 February 1994, at the Rose office.[6] Clark has since denied that any documents were improperly shredded, saying the firm had "actively made every effort to preserve all files" connected to Whitewater.[7]

The Congressional Record also reflects that during the 1992 presidential campaign, three current or former

Rose employees told Congressmen that couriers from Rose were summoned to the governor's mansion by Hillary Rodham Clinton, who personally gave them records to be taken to the Rose office and shredded. This was apparently Rodham Clinton's response to a report in the *New York Times* on 8 March 1992 that the Clintons were involved in the Whitewater deal. Rose couriers made no less than six more runs during the campaign to pick up additional files at the governor's mansion for shredding. The records were sealed in unmarked envelopes.

In all, through the 3 November general election, dozens of boxes of files belonging to Foster, Rodham Clinton, and Webb Hubbell were shredded. In fact, James and Susan McDougal have said they personally turned over all of their Whitewater files to Rodham Clinton at the mansion in December 1987, pursuant to her request.[8] At a press conference in April 1994, the First Lady denied making any such request. Mrs. McDougal, however, told Robert Fiske she had put all of the Whitewater records she had in a box, and that one of her brothers, William or James Henley, had taken the box to the mansion with specific instructions that it was to be given to Mrs. Clinton. The Henleys were both officers with Madison Guaranty Savings & Loan.[9]

All of Foster's Whitewater files, and some other files containing information about bond issues in Arkansas, appear to have been removed from his office in the west wing of the White House shortly after his death. They were sent upstairs to the third floor residence of the First Family and locked in a storage closet where other personal papers and effects are kept. Margaret Williams had a key to the closet and permitted Clinton counsel Robert Barnett to pick up some of the files five days later.[10]

In December 1993, the White House disclosed for the first time that "a Whitewater file" had been found in

Foster's office. At the time, the White House failed to reveal Williams' involvement or the fact that the files had been locked in the third-floor storage closet. The only information divulged was by Communications Director Mark Gearan, who said merely that certain files were sent to Barnett, the Clintons' personal attorney. In fairness to Gearan, he divulged what was apparently the only information he had at the time, as Nussbaum, Williams, and Thomasson are obviously very good at keeping certain matters confidential. For their part, the president and the First Lady have denied even looking at any of the files culled from Foster's office during the several days they were in the closet in the First Family's residence.[11]

Because of her rather shady background, one has to wonder exactly what role Patsy Thomasson has played as White House director of administration. She is obviously in a very high-level, high-security position in the White House (she's in charge of security clearance and visitors' passes). Moreover, as one of only three individuals initially allowed into Vince Foster's office the day he died, to the exclusion of law enforcement agents, Ms. Thomasson must be regarded by the president and First Lady as a very trustworthy individual.

Perhaps less trustworthy is Thomasson's close friend and former business associate, Danny Ray "Dan" Lasater. And, any discussion of Thomasson must, of necessity, involve Lasater. He became one of Bill Clinton's closest friends and political supporters in the 1970s and 1980s in Arkansas.

Lasater moved to Little Rock from Kentucky in the seventies and made a fortune in the food-service industry. He started a low-budget restaurant chain called Ponderosa Steak House and, through franchising, quickly became a millionaire. An owner of thoroughbreds, Lasater apparently came to know Bill Clinton after meeting Clinton's mother, a nurse anesthetist named

Virginia Kelley, and his half-brother, Roger Clinton, at a horse-racing track in Hot Springs. Their friendship grew, and Lasater became a strong political ally of Bill Clinton. During the 1980s, the Clintons were frequent guests at Angel Fire, Lasater's seventeen thousand-acre resort in the mountains of New Mexico.

In time, Lasater formed a bond-brokerage firm called Lasater & Company. Headquartered in Little Rock, the company would eventually receive millions of dollars from state-backed bond issues in Arkansas in the eighties. These bond issues were facilitated by an organization formed under Clinton's direction in 1985 and known as ADFA (the Arkansas Development Finance Authority).[12]

In 1985, at a time when Lasater was under investigation and was about to be arrested and charged with possession of cocaine with intent to distribute, Bill Clinton rewarded Lasater & Company with a $30.2 million bond issue to modernize the Arkansas State Police radio system. Documents from the Nashville office of the Regional Organized Crime Center dated 15 May 1985 contain a request for information on Lasater in connection with alleged narcotics trafficking via aircraft. The documents also suggest Lasater may have had ties to organized crime at the time. Furthermore, documents on file in federal court in Little Rock reflect the time frame and basis for Lasater's indictment on federal drug-trafficking charges in 1986.[13]

Whether or not then-Gov. Bill Clinton had actual knowledge of Lasater's drug dealing at the time the radio system bond issue was made may be entirely irrelevant. What is relevant, however, is that in Arkansas in the mid-1980s, funds for these types of projects routinely came from the State Treasury, but, because this funding was in the form of a bond offer, Lasater & Company was able to reap a handsome $750,000 underwriter's fee. The governor's signature on each bond issue was required by law. During the time Lasater was being investigated for drug dealing, his brokerage handled over $664 million in Arkansas state bond issues and grossed $1.6 million in brokerage fees, all authorized by Bill Clinton.[14]

In December 1986, Lasater was sentenced to thirty months in prison on the cocaine charges leveled by the federal grand jury. He apparently served only four months in a halfway house, and two additional months under "house arrest." Lasater was pardoned by Gov. Bill Clinton in November 1990.

While Lasater was serving his time on the federal charges, his brokerage was run by its executive vice president, Patsy Thomasson. She was also the former chairman of the Arkansas Highway Commission, having been appointed to that position by Bill Clinton.[15] Perhaps because of her relationship with Lasater, Thomasson's name is said to appear in the files of various law enforcement agencies as being involved in drug trafficking.[16]

After his release, Lasater became chairman of Phoenix Mortgage Company, a Little Rock mortgage brokerage. Some time later, Patsy Thomasson was listed in legal documents as president of Phoenix Group, Inc., a holding company which controls Phoenix Mortgage.[17]

Lasater and Thomasson have obviously maintained a close working relationship for years, despite Lasater's drug conviction. However, it appears that Patsy Thomasson's loyalty and trustworthiness begin and end with her working relationships and political connections, because she completely turned her back on at least one Lasater investor when he needed her most.

Dennis Patrick, a former clerk with a Kentucky state court, was lured into investing with Lasater & Company in 1985 after Lasater broker Steven Love, a friend of Patrick's from high school, invited Patrick to join him in an expense-paid, deep-sea fishing trip off the Louisiana coast. During that trip, Love spent most of his waking

hours trying to convince Patrick of the sagacity of investing with Lasater. Love told Patrick that accounts could
be established in his name and that he would reap gen-
erous profits from investments made through those accounts. Patrick was extremely skeptical, having a net
worth of approximately $60,000 at the time, but agreed
to place his life savings of $21,000 in Love's hands.
Patrick would later learn, through FBI agents investigating the Whitewater-Madison Guaranty connection, that
nearly $110 million (including $23 million for the purchase of Federal Home Loan Mortgage Corporation
general revenue bonds) was passed through Patrick &
Associates, based in Williamsburg, Kentucky, between
July 1985 and February 1986. Patrick had nothing to do
with the formation of Patrick & Associates. When the
Internal Revenue Service besieged him, Patrick called on
Thomasson for help and was assured that everything
would be fine.[18]

Despite her assurances to the contrary, after Patrick
placed the call to Thomasson, at least three assassination
attempts were made on his life. All three occurred in
1987. The first, a firebombing of his home in
Williamsburg, followed an appearance made by Patrick
in a lawsuit filed by Lasater in connection with alleged
unpaid broker's commissions. Four men were later arrested on various charges, including attempted murder,
attempted arson, and conspiracy. Patrick is now reported
to be in hiding, with his wife and children.[19]

In late 1994, Lasater was rumored to have been
living near Paron, Arkansas, in a lodge nestled in a
densely wooded seventy-three-hundred-acre tract purchased from International Paper Co., by Southeast Investments, Inc. The president of Southeast is Kenneth
Shemin, a partner in the Rose Law Firm.

Since Lasater moved there, residents of Paron have
noticed a vast increase in aircraft and trucking activity in
the area. Planes land, then later on trucks and jeeps

leave the area where the planes landed. However, such activity may simply be in keeping with Lasater's affinity for aircraft and flight. In the early 1980s, the U.S. Drug Enforcement Agency began to build a file on Lasater, based in part on intelligence indicating he might be working with the notorious drug trafficker and gun smuggler, Barry Seal. During that time period, Seal flew hundreds of flights in and out of Mena, Arkansas, carrying weapons to Central America and returning with drugs and sacks of cash. Lasater also had a habit of flying to Latin America. A March 1984 memo, allegedly contained in Lasater's DEA file, reported that White House staffer Patsy Thomasson had been a "designated passenger on private flights with Lasater to South America and Latin America."[20]

When such facts about the White House chief of administration can easily be discerned through a fairly simple investigation, the procedures employed by the Clinton administration in checking the backgrounds of prospective appointees become extremely suspect. Yet, Ms. Thomasson, and others like her, have been welcomed with open arms.

Endnotes

1. Sessions had publicly stated he would resign as soon as his replacement was confirmed by the Senate, so that the bureau would have a director at all times.

2. Congressional Record, vol. 140, no. 104, House of Representatives, Tuesday, 2 August 1994.

3. Ibid.

4. Sessions had arranged a meeting with Gary Coker, a Waco attorney who'd previously represented Koresh and believed he knew him well enough to reason with him. Reno disagreed and decided to use CS gas (tear gas), based in part on "historical evidence" that children were being

abused in the compound. The day after the raid, Sessions appeared on national television and explained that there had been "no direct evidence of contemporaneous child abuse" at the compound, all of which was true if FBI intelligence was accurate. Reno was livid. Sessions remained FBI director a few more months, until 19 July 1993, the day before Vince Foster committed suicide. See, "U.S. Department of Justice, Report to the Deputy Attorney General on the Events at Waco, Texas," 28 February to 19 April 1993.

5. Congressional Record, 2 August 1994.

6. Ibid.

7. *Washington Times*, National Weekly Edition, Special Report, 12 December 1994.

8. Ibid.

9. Ibid.

10. Ibid.

11. Ibid.

12. *Washington Times*, "Whitewater probe eyes alleged laundering of drug profiles," 6 June 1994.

13. A federal grand jury indictment was handed down in the form of a true bill, in 1986, in the U.S. District Court for the Eastern District of Arkansas, in a case captioned *United States of America v. Dan R. Lasater*, no. LR-CR-86-21 U.S.C. sec. 846. In the indictment, Lasater was formally charged with a continuing, willful conspiracy, "from on or about December 15, 1980 and continuing to on or about September 15, 1985," with Roger Clinton, among others, to "possess with the intent to distribute cocaine, a Schedule II Narcotic Controlled Substance, a violation of Title 21, United States Code, section 841(a), thereby violating Title 21, United States Code, section 846." The information about the Regional Organized Crime Center in Nashville, has not been confirmed. Its source is Patrick Matrisciana, *The Clinton Chronicles Book*. (Hemet, CA: Jeremiah Books, 1994.)

14. *Washington Times*, 6 June 1994.

15. L.J. Davis, *New Republic*, 4 April 1994.

16. Matrisciana, *Clinton Chronicles*, 62.

17. *Washington Times*, 6 June 1994.

18. Ibid.

19. Ibid.

20. Matrisciana, *Clinton Chronicles*, 182.

Chapter Four

Barry Seal and the Mena Connection

Wednesday, 19 February 1986, had been a typical winter day in south Louisiana, overcast and cold, but not unbearable. Barry Seal wasn't concerned about the weather anyway; the late model Cadillac Sedan deVille he was driving had all of the creature comforts and amenities befitting a big-time drug trafficker. Shortly before 6:00 P.M., the forty-six-year-old Seal wheeled the yellow Cadillac into the parking lot of the Salvation Army Community Treatment Center in Baton Rouge. He had been ordered by a federal judge to spend his nights there as part of his sentence after pleading guilty to money-laundering and cocaine-trafficking charges, in connection with a $168 million drug deal.[1]

Two days earlier, a Colombian national named Bernardo Antonio Vasquez had rented a room at a motel near the halfway house. The balcony of the motel gave the second-floor occupants an unobstructed view of the lot where Seal customarily parked his car. Two other Colombians, Luis Carlos Quintero-Cruz and Miguel Velez, shared Vasquez's room.

No one knows exactly why, but for some reason, after pulling the Cadillac into its normal parking place, Seal, dressed in his customary olive-drab flight suit, and wearing his amber Ray Ban aviator sunglasses, sat in the car that evening a lot longer than was his usual custom. As the light of day began to fade, a gray Buick driven by Velez raced into the parking lot, pulling within a few feet of Seal's vehicle, on the driver's side. Cruz and Vasquez were in the Buick with Velez and were armed with 9 millimeter automatic weapons. As the car came to a screeching halt, Cruz and Vasquez sprang from the front and rear passenger-side seats, spraying the Cadillac with bullets, gangland style. They immediately hopped back into the Buick and sped away, nearly running over an eyewitness.

According to the East Baton Rouge Parish Coroner, Dr. Hypolite Landry, and the report of detectives with the Baton Rouge City Police, seven rounds fired from an automatic weapon known as a Mac-10 struck Seal in the head and upper body. He died instantly.[2]

Who Was Barry Seal?

Hired by TWA, at age twenty-seven, Adler Berriman "Barry" Seal was the youngest pilot in U.S. history to fly a commercial airliner. He was also the youngest pilot to be promoted to captain of the crew of a Boeing 707, and later of a Boeing 747.[3] A former Green Beret, Seal became one of TWA's top pilots.

Barry Seal, and his younger brothers, Benjy and Wendell, grew up in a typical American household. They played ball in the yard of the one-story white frame house on Lover's Lane, a shady street in a quiet neighborhood. They also souped up old cars in the garage behind the house. But, Barry's first love was flying. When he was a boy, he would frequently ride his bicycle to a local private airport two miles from his house, where he would lean on the chain-link fence and watch small planes take off and land.

Eventually, Barry joined the local Civil Air Patrol and learned to fly Piper Cubs. In high school, while his classmates were riding buses to out-of-town football games, Barry would often fly to the games in "barnstorming" fashion, landing wherever he could find a smooth, flat surface. He attended Louisiana State University for one year, but decided that he didn't need a college degree to fly airplanes. After a military hitch, he returned to Baton Rouge and started flying again.

While flying for TWA in the early 1970s, Seal did a little "moonlighting." The moonlighting, which involved smuggling operations, earned him a reputation as a risk-taking soldier of fortune. In 1972, he and eight others were convicted in federal court in New Orleans of running guns and explosives to Mexico.[4] The conviction was overturned on appeal, but he lost his job with TWA. Between his salary as a tenured pilot with TWA and the money he made as a gun runner, Seal had gotten used to a rather high standard of living. With the TWA money gone, he looked for other means of subsidizing his income. Smuggling drugs was the most lucrative business Seal had heard of, and he owned his own airplanes, so he offered his services as a contract pilot.

He started out smuggling marijuana, but he was apprehended and jailed in Honduras in December 1979. However, as fate would have it, Seal was placed in the same jail cell as Emile Camp, a pilot from Slidell, Louisiana, who had also been arrested for smuggling. Obviously, Seal and Camp had a lot in common and plenty of time to talk. After their release, Seal contacted Camp, and he became Seal's partner, copilot, and best friend. They remained partners until Camp's untimely death in a plane crash just north of Mena, Arkansas, on 20 February 1985. They had worked steadily together, as DEA informants from the spring of 1984 till February 1985.[5]

On the flight home from Honduras, Seal met Carlos Bustamonte, a Miami car dealer. Bustamonte was also associated with the Ochoa family of the infamous Medellin drug cartel. Bustamonte later explained to Seal that Nicaragua was an excellent place to engage in dope smuggling because the Communist Sandinistas provided the cartel with a safe harbor for the transfer of Colombian cocaine from one airplane to another when the final destination was the United States.[6]

In the late 1970s and early 1980s, the Medellin cartel (named after the city in Colombia which was the center of activity for most of those associated with the drug trade) supplied at least 75 percent of the cocaine smuggled into the U.S. One traffic route was through Miami, often by way of Port-au-Prince, the capital of Haiti. Another was through the little town of Mena, in western Arkansas.

The Ochoa family cartel, led at the time by Jorge Ochoa-Vasquez, the son of Fabio Ochoa-Vasquez, a prominent Colombian cattle farmer, found Seal to be such a reliable pilot that they paid him to make dozens of cocaine runs. Seal flew fifty cocaine-smuggling and money-laundering missions between 1981 and 1983 for the Medellin cartel. He normally received a commission for his work. It wasn't unusual for him to transport up to $20 million in cash in exchange for a commission of 5 percent of that amount.[7]

But, in February 1984, Seal was convicted in federal court in south Florida for possession with intent to distribute Quaaludes. At the time he was also under indictment in the same federal jurisdiction on thirteen counts of possession with intent to distribute phenobarbitol, Demerol, and Quaaludes. With the threat of a lengthy prison term looming ominously over his head, the free-spirited Seal decided to cooperate with authorities and become an informant.

For some time before his problems surfaced in Florida, Seal had been making cocaine and money laundering runs to rural Arkansas.[8] Micah Morrison, writing in the 18 October 1994 edition of the *Wall Street Journal*, says Seal actually began operating out of the Mena (Arkansas) Intermountain Regional Airport in 1981. Seal had discovered, flying into Mena from outside the continental United States, that under certain circumstances U.S. Customs agents at the airport did not inspect aircraft. Seal soon purchased a hangar and began to operate a new business, Rich Mountain Aviation, Inc.

According to Russell Welch, Seal admitted in late 1985 that aircraft were being "retrofitted" with cargo doors, bladder tands and special plumbing, and fuel and navigational system modifications in the Rich Mountain hangar between 1981 and 1985. The main purpose of the modifications was to facilitate long-distance nonstop flights to Central and South America from Arkansas. A secondary purpose was to avoid U.S. Customs scrutiny. Crews, passengers, and cargo apparently didn't have to go through Customs if the aircraft was landing at Mena for retrofitting. Welch was an investigator for the Arkansas State Police Criminal Investigations Division, taking part in Seal's prosecution in federal court in Baton Rouge on drug-trafficking and money-laundering charges. He attended one of Seal's depositions on 27 December 1985, and heard Seal make these admissions.[9]

Barry Seal, Federal Informant

During 1985, the Ochoa cartel became increasingly concerned about recent seizures of their drugs by U.S. government agents and made major adjustments in flight schedules, contacts, and drug-drop locations.[10] Jorge Ochoa would soon discover that Barry Seal, whom the cartel had long trusted, was playing a significant role in the cartel's looming problems.

Because of the overwhelming evidence against him, Seal had been forced to plead guilty in 1984 to drug-trafficking charges in an unrelated federal court proceeding in south Florida. Through a rather circuitous route, Seal turned DEA informant under the threat of additional prosecution on drug-trafficking and money-laundering charges in the federal cases filed against him in Miami and Baton Rouge.

Seal was indicted by a federal grand jury in Baton Rouge on 20 December 1984. He was charged with possession of 462 pounds of cocaine, a Schedule II federally controlled narcotic dangerous substance, and for conspiring with others to distribute that cocaine between 1 June 1982 and 1 January 1983. Those were alleged violations of Title 21, Sections 841 and 846, of the United States Code. Seal was also charged with concealing material facts from the Internal Revenue Service about the existence, source, or origin, of $51,006.64 and for failure to file currency transaction reports on amounts in excess of $10,000. The failure to report and file the proper forms allegedly violated Title 31, Section 1081 of the United State Code; Title 31, Section 103.22 of the Code of Federal Regulations; and Title 18, Section 1001-2 of the United States Code. According to the indictment, Seal had made unlawful transfers in the amount of $51,006.64 by purchasing a cashier's check in that amount with $8,656.64 in cash and five cashier's checks in amounts of less than $10,000 each.[11]

It is well documented that Seal was one of the top five drug smugglers in the United States.[12] He first admitted this under oath before the President's Commission on Organized Crime. He next admitted it under oath in DEA intelligence reports. And, he admitted it during cross examination in the Saunders trial in September 1984.[13] In early 1984, months before the actual indictment was handed down in Baton Rouge, Seal had realized that it was only a matter of time before the death knell sounded on his $25 million-a-year drug-trafficking operation.

Special drug prosecutors Bradley C. Myers and Albert J. Winters, Jr., with the New Orleans office of the U.S.

Attorney's Organized Crime Strike Force, knew all of that and had been breathing down Seal's neck for months. In March 1984, frustrated by numerous vain attempts to talk personally with U.S. Attorney Stanford Bardwell, who was prosecuting the case in Baton Rouge, the now-desperate Seal contacted the Vice-Presidential Task Force in Washington, D.C., and made arrangements to meet with them a day or two later. On March 24, Vice-Presidential Aide Jim Howell met with Seal, as did DEA Special Agents Frank White and Bill Kennedy. The DEA was obviously delighted when Seal agreed to become an informant. Agents White and Kennedy quickly arranged for Seal to meet with DEA Special Agents Robert Jura and Ernest Jacobson in Miami. Seal kept his appointment with Jura and Jacobson five days after his meeting with the task force. He would work closely with the two agents in setting up a sting operation involving the Medellin-based Ochoa cartel.[14]

Now officially known as Confidential Informant No. SGI-84-0028, Seal told the DEA about an upcoming smuggling trip in which he planned to haul "3000 kilos" of cocaine "from the Jorge Ochoa smuggling group." During his initial conversation with Jura and Jacobson, and to insure against being double-crossed, Seal reiterated what he told White and Kennedy during the meeting in Washington: he would be "willing to cooperate" with the DEA in exchange "for their assistance in helping [him] out with [his] sentences in south Florida."[15] After being reassured by the two special agents, Seal went forward with his plans to make the trip to Medellin. He invited fellow drug smuggler Felix Dixon Bates to join him.

Things went smoothly in Medellin, as Seal and Bates met with Jorge Ochoa. After the two returned, Seal gave a full debriefing to Jura and Jacobson. His next DEA-related trip was to Panama. Seal then made a series of drug-smuggling flights, all with DEA approval. The information gleaned during these trips led to the eventual arrest and extradition arrest of Norman Saunders, Stafford Missick, Aulden Smith, Andre Fournier, and, ultimately, the Panamanian dictator, Gen. Manuel Noreiga. Seal also gave the DEA valuable additional information on Medellin drug lord, Pablo Escobar.[16]

The Saunders case had enormous implications for the South American drug-trafficking trade. At the time of their extradition and prosecution, billions of dollars in drug money had already been laundered through banks affiliated with and operated by BCCI (the Bank of Commerce and Credit International) in the tiny Caribbean island chain known as the Turks and Caicos. Norman Saunders and Stafford Missick were high-ranking public officials in the islands. Saunders had been the government's chief minister, and Missick was the minister of Commerce and Development. Co-defendant Aulden Smith had been a police officer in Grand Turk, and co-defendant Andre Fournier had assisted the others in making connections with BCCI and the Colombian cartels for years.

The Turks and Caicos Islands lie at the southeast end of the Bahamas. Of the thirty islands in the tiny chain, only six are inhabited. Those six islands contain a total of 193 square miles of land. About twelve thousand people live in the islands, mainly in the capital of Grand Turk. Although the economy is officially based on the fishing industry and a few salt mines, the Turks and Caicos boasted an exclusive Club Med resort in the eighties.

Barry Seal had friends in the islands, one of whom was Eric Arthur. Arthur lived on South Caicos, where he ran a smuggling-related business. He stored, bought, and sold aircraft used in smuggling, introduced smugglers to each other, and helped them make connections. According to Seal, he and Arthur had made "a couple of hundred thousand [dollars]" together over the years. Arthur

had a very large airstrip and a clean spacious aircraft
hangar on a tract of land he leased from the Turks and
Caicos government. Seal used both frequently. When
Arthur was killed in 1984, Seal began paying the lease
on the property, under the pretext of helping Arthur's
widow, who was still liable for lease payments. At that
point, if they hadn't known it before, the government
now knew who Seal was and would soon learn what he
was about.[17]

Seal and his copilot, Emile Camp, who had also
become a DEA informant in 1984 to avoid prosecution,
flew to Grand Turk Island on 2 January 1985, in part to
arrange the sale of a Beechcraft 18 airplane to Leocadida
Moreno. While in the islands, Seal was introduced to
Aulden Smith and, at the DEA's behest, paid Smith two
thousand dollars to be introduced to Norman Saunders.
Seal made his request all the more convincing by arranging to return to the islands in a couple of weeks to look
at a DC-3 he might want to buy with Smith's assistance.[18]

When Seal returned to the Turks and Caicos in February, he initially met with Smith. During their conversation, it became obvious to Seal that Smith knew he was
a drug smuggler. Since the cat was out of the bag, Seal
asked Smith what could be done to better "protect" his
airplanes that were being stored periodically in the islands. Smith pointed him in Norman Saunders' direction and helped arrange a meeting with Saunders at
Arthur's hangar.

The next day, Saunders drove up in a white Lincoln
Continental Mark IV, accompanied by two bodyguards
and a third man dressed in a white seersucker suit. After
exchanging pleasantries with Saunders, the Turks and
Caicos government's chief minister, Seal got to the point
and asked Saunders if he was interested in participating
in Seal's drug-smuggling operation, for a share of the
profits, of course. Seal needed the protection, and
Saunders and his friends could use the money. At the

same time, Seal was introduced to the man in the white suit, Stafford Missick, minister of Commerce and Finance in the islands. Both Smith and Missick were interested in Seal's proposal and were given cash advances on the spot out of what Seal called his "trafficker fund" (money provided by the DEA for its informants' use) for "transportation expenses" associated with a meeting arranged for Miami in March.[19]

On 3 March 1985, as scheduled, Seal met with Smith, Missick, Andre Fournier, and Nigel Bowe at a Miami hotel. Bowe was a well-known lawyer and drug smuggler in the region. Seal had known of him for "many, many years." Saunders couldn't make the Miami meeting, but Seal was assured he would be part of any deals the five men might strike. The entire meeting was videotaped by DEA agents in the next room. After the details were discussed and "a division of labor" was decided on, Seal promised that the islanders would divide at least $1,250,000 annually. Fournier had the most work to do, so he was to receive $375,000 a year. He'd had profitable dealings with Colombian drug lord Pablo Escobar for a number of years. He agreed to use that connection for the benefit of the new joint venture. They agreed that $250,000 would be applied to cover expenses, such as fuel, storage, and lease fees, and the balance would be divided evenly among Saunders, Smith, Missick, and Bowe, based mainly on their promise to prepare and sign documents and to look the other way at certain crucial times. The meeting ended, appropriately, with smiles, handshakes, and *hasta la vistas*. Little did the islanders know that the evidence elicited from the videotape of this meeting would ultimately lead to the arrest, extradition, and conviction of three of the men present.[20]

"Uncle Sam Wants You"

Throughout 1984, Barry Seal continued to fly to Colombia, Nicaragua, Panama, the Caymans, and the

Turks and Caicos as a DEA informant doing business with Jorge Ochoa, Pablo Escobar, and Carlos Lehder, all members of the Medellin cartel. Seal admitted under oath smuggling at least fifteen hundred pounds of cocaine during the six months between May and November of that year. His favorite mode of transportation for these flights was a modified military C-123 aircraft he affectionately referred to as The Fat Lady.

A C-123 is so large that vehicles can be driven into its fuselage for transport. In Seal's words, "You could easily drive a couple of Jeeps and bigger vehicles into [The Fat Lady] and be on your way." The Fat Lady was camouflaged. In addition to flying the huge aircraft in and out of the Mena, Arkansas, Intermountain Regional Airport, Seal used a private airport in Opa-Locka, Florida, from time to time, for the same basic reason that had initially attracted him to Mena: no U.S. Customs agents were there to examine crews, passengers, or cargo if the aircraft was landing for retrofitting.[21]

The absence of Customs agents in Mena also meant illegal retrofitting could take place with little or no concern for the repercussions normally associated with unlawful activity. According to both Seal and Terry Reed, who claims to have been a CIA "asset" in the 1980s and who flew with Seal in and out of Mena on numerous occasions, The Fat Lady was equipped by the CIA with surveillance cameras for a sting operation in Nicaragua involving the Sandinistas and the Medellin cartel. A drug shipment transfer in Nicaragua was in fact videotaped with The Fat Lady's surveillance camera. President Reagan used some of the footage on national television to reveal the involvement of the Sandinistas and the Medellin cartel in drug trafficking and to demonstrate the need for stronger drug enforcement.[22]

Although he spent most of his time out of state, Barry Seal maintained close ties with friends and family in Louisiana. He owned a camp on the oak-studded banks of the Amite River, in swampy Ascension Parish,

near the village of French Settlement. He also bought
over a thousand acres of land across a gravel road from
the camp and had a large portion of it cleared of trees
and brush, leveled, and sodded with a carpet of thick
Bermuda grass. The cleared area is over a mile long and
is between five hundred and seven hundred feet wide. A
sign located at one end of the property, bearing the
standard FAA announcement that the field is an aircraft
landing strip, and forbidding trespassing or tampering
with aircraft, remains to this day. The sign boldly reflects
that "A.B. Seal" is the owner of the airstrip. Seal specifically bought the property and made the improvements
to accommodate The Fat Lady.

When he was cross-examined in the Saunders trial,
Seal didn't deny that he "had worked on CIA-sponsored
activities in Nicaragua," and he admitted that "the CIA
installed the cameras in the C-123," which were used in
the Sandinista sting operation.[23] In fact, in November
1984, Seal released an hour-long videotape publicizing
his CIA and DEA-related smuggling activities. The tape,
entitled "Uncle Sam Wants You," was narrated by John
Camp, who is now an investigative reporter for CNN.[24]
At the time, Camp was an investigative reporter for
WBRZ-TV, the Baton Rouge ABC affiliate.

Seal testified in the Saunders trial that "Uncle Sam
Wants You" was produced to publicize his covert activities because he was afraid that if he continued to work
in the obscurity of the drug-trafficking trade, he might
be killed by the CIA or DEA, and those investigating his
death might try to create the illusion that thugs hired by
some Medellin drug lord had assassinated him. In fact,
in the federal proceedings in Baton Rouge, Seal's lawyers filed pleadings containing the following language:

> The defendant [Seal] has been restrained by Court
> order in Florida, and so has the prosecutor here,
> from fully outlining to the Court the danger to
> the defendant and the activities of the defendant

on behalf of various Federal agencies, including the D.E.A. and C.I.A., and this has prevented frank discussion regarding the plea bargain and terms of probation.[25]

The "plea bargain" and "probation" referred to the plea agreement Seal was finally able to reach with federal prosecutors in Baton Rouge, in November 1984, just before the grand jury indictment was formally handed down. U.S. Attorney Stanford Bardwell prepared a letter on 19 November 1984. Some of the more pertinent portions of the letter are as follows:

> The Government anticipates bringing an indictment to a grand jury . . . charging the defendant [Seal] with a violation of one count of conspiracy to possess with intent to distribute cocaine. . . . In addition, the indictment will contain one count of causing financial institutions not to file currency transaction reports (CTRs). . . . Should the grand jury return the indictment, the Government agrees to allow the defendant to plead guilty to the two-count indictment.

> This plea agreement is predicated upon the fact that the defendant cooperates totally, including agreeing to submit to debriefing whenever and wherever requested by Special Agents of the Government and Department of Justice attorneys investigating criminal matters.

> * * * * *

> The Government and defense further agree . . . that the defendant will receive a concurrent sentence as to Count I not to exceed the ultimate sentence he receives in a pending proceeding . . . in the Southern District of Florida.[26]

On 20 December 1984, the grand jury did in fact return an indictment, and U.S. District Judge Frank Polozola signed a Judgment and Probation/Commitment

Order in Seal's criminal proceeding. That order, which
for reasons discussed below would ultimately become
Seal's death warrant, reflected that he wouldn't do any
jail time for the cocaine charges, but instead would pay
a fine of twenty-five thousand dollars. As to count two
(the tax-related charges), the court's order placed Seal
on probation for five years and fined him ten thousand
dollars. Seal was also ordered to report address changes
to the U.S. attorney, and his right to travel outside the
court's jurisdiction was restricted.[27]

At the time the order was signed, and in the weeks
that followed, Seal continued to work with the government as an informant, although his smuggling activity
had been substantially curtailed by Judge Polozola's order. In response to a complaint by his federal probation
officer, Lionell Jardell, that Seal wasn't cooperating
enough in the pre-sentencing investigation, one of Seal's
lawyers, Lewis Unglesby, reminded Jardell that Seal was
working constantly "under government supervision in
dangerous and difficult situations."[28]

Polozola's order also contained certain "special conditions." These required Seal to carry a telephone pag-
ing device, file monthly financial reports, and abstain
from all contact with a co-defendant named Gary Seville.
However, it was the final special condition that Seal's
lawyers would object to most strenuously, and for good
reason. That condition was as follows:

> (6) The defendant [Seal] shall reside at the Salva-
> tion Army Community Treatment Center, 7361
> Airline Highway, Baton Rouge, Louisiana, for a
> period of six (6) months.

Seal was ordered to report to the Salvation Army
center on a future date to be determined by the federal
probation office. Seal's lawyers immediately protested
by filing motions averring that, in an effort to fulfill the
terms of the plea bargain, Seal was engaged in activities

which could place him in serious danger if he were housed at a halfway house.

Despite the plea agreement, U.S. Attorney Stanford Bardwell had to prepare for the worst. If he ultimately had to prosecute Seal, he wanted Albert J. Winters, Jr., the supervisory trial attorney for the federal government's New Orleans Organized Crime Strike Force, to testify against Seal. But, because Winters was participating in a trial on 4 January, the arraignment date initially set by the court, Bardwell sought and was given a continuance until the next week, 8 January 1985. Seal's arraignment proceeded as scheduled on that date.

Al Winters did in fact testify at the arraignment regarding Seal's criminal activities, telling the court that the charges in the indictment were based on solid evidence. A minute entry on that date reflected that Seal would "remain at liberty under the terms of his original bond."[29] Unfortunately, the very liberty Barry Seal sought, and for which he had posted a $250,000 unsecured bond, made him an easy target for assassins.

In light of the manner in which Seal was killed, what is perhaps most incredible about the way his prosecution in federal courts in Florida and Louisiana was handled, is that key DEA and CIA agents in both locales apparently didn't know much about each others' activities, contacts, or plans; unless, of course, Seal's assassination in February 1986 was advanced and facilitated by the very agencies for which he'd agreed to furnish information. That was certainly Seal's fear when he produced "Uncle Sam Wants You," and it may have been well founded.

The Mena Connection

Ambrose Evans-Pritchard reported in the 9 October 1994 *London Sunday Telegraph* that the diary of former Arkansas State Police Investigator Russell Welch contained the following entry on 4 June 1985: "[An agent from the DEA] informed me in strictest confidence that it was believed, within his department, that Barry Seal is [*sic*] flying weapons to Central and South America. In return he is [*sic*] allowed to smuggle what he wanted back into the United States."

In his cross-examination in the Saunders trial, Seal stopped short of admitting culpability for anything more than smuggling explosives into Mexico in the early 1970s.[30] However, it was commonly rumored (and with good reason) in both Louisiana and Arkansas in the 1980s that Barry Seal was engaged in the arms trade as well as being a cocaine trafficker. Some, like Terry Reed, who claims to have been a CIA "asset" himself in the 1980s, have gone much further.[31]

According to Reed and his coauthor, John Cummings, retired U.S. Marine Lt. Col. Oliver North was working for the CIA in Oklahoma and Arkansas in the 1980s. Using the code name John Cathey, North is said to have orchestrated a complicated scheme by which the Nicaraguan Contra Rebels' freedom-fighting activities could be financed, and by which they could be armed with fully automatic M-16-type rifles.

The financing scheme was essentially as follows. Individuals who wanted to help the Contras would allow big-ticket items like boats, helicopters, small planes, and sport/utility vehicles to mysteriously disappear. The CIA or its contractors would actually abscond with the items and convert them for use by the Contras. Through a prearranged agreement, the insured property owner would file a loss claim, be paid by his insurance carrier (so his only loss was of the item, not its value), and the insurance carrier would then get the benefit of certain "tax breaks" which allegedly increased the "net income for the losing insurance company" due to increased underwriting losses. Insurance companies with loss reserves could sell future claims to other companies, "giving the first company immediate income from the purchase, and from the unused claim money." In purchasing the future claims, the second company would be provided with "instant tax write-offs through mandatory, tax-exempt cash set aside requirements."[32] Ironically, if such a scheme really was in place, the federal government was in effect subsidizing the Contras through tax deductions, in violation of its own laws.

The reason the scheme was so complicated, according to Reed and Cummings, is that the federal government couldn't legally fund the Contras without congressional approval, as such actions were prohibited by the Boland Amendment.[33] Of course, there were other ways to fund the Freedom Fighters, including the National Endowment for the Preservation of Liberty, Gomez International, Miller Communications, International Business Communications, and Lake Resources, all organizations involved at one level or another in receiving and redistributing money for Nicaragua.[34]

Although there are conflicting reports, it appears Seal was originally recruited by the CIA as a "subcontractor" to fly arms and other contraband to the Nicaraguan Freedom Fighters, beginning sometime in 1983 after he allegedly met with Terry Reed to discuss gun-smuggling activities. Reed claims the meeting with Seal was arranged by Oliver North (aka John Cathey).[35] According to Reed and Cummings, during this first meeting, Seal advised that Iver Johnson's Arms, Inc., a New Jersey company that manufactured weapons and weapons parts, had moved to Arkansas. Another company, Brodix Manufacturing, had the machinery to cast the parts (lower receiver housings and carrier assemblies) necessary to convert semiautomatic into automatic rifles, especially M-16s. Johnson's could make everything but the special parts. Brodix would take the greater risk and manufacture the conversion kits.[36]

For his part, Seal may not have known that a number of weapons-manufacturing and sales firms were operating in Arkansas in the 1980s. These included Nessard Gun Parts, an Illinois company dealing in semi-automatic weapons; Sarco, Inc., a New Jersey company known mainly as a retailer, but which also sold conversion kits in Arkansas in the 1980s; Olympic Arms, Inc., a Washington retailer handling semiautomatics; Center Fire Systems, of Kentucky, which continues to do business in Arkansas to this day; and Shooters Equipment, a South Carolina manufacturer handling conversion kits in the eighties.

Many individuals in Arkansas, and elsewhere, bought weapons and conversion kits from those companies, sometimes in large quantities. But, the obvious difference between Nessard, Sarco, and the others and Iver Johnson's and Brodix was that the physical plants of the last two were located in Arkansas. In theory, that meant the state of Arkansas was able to exact tax revenues from them. In practice, it meant they would be given a few tax breaks, in addition to other incentives, for cooperating with people like Seal. A great deal of corporate naivete and ignorance on the part of state government was to be expected in Bill Clinton's Arkansas, with respect to certain business transactions where Barry Seal, Iver Johnson's, and Brodix were involved, as long as the appropriate fees were paid to the right parties.

Gun smuggling, especially the brand the CIA and Seal were engaged in in Arkansas and elsewhere in the 1980s, was risky business. Not only did the smuggler have to be careful in terms of how he dealt with those on the receiving end of each shipment, he had to constantly look over his shoulder to see what the ATF (Bureau of Alcohol, Tobacco, and Firearms) was doing. Converting a Colt AR-15 semiautomatic rifle into a fully automatic M-16 is a relatively easy task. It's a matter of modifying the receiver and replacing the internal parts in the carrier assembly. That was what the white supremacist cult, CSA, was doing in Arkansas in the early-to-mid-1980s. It's also what the Branch Davidians were doing at Mt. Carmel, their compound outside Waco, Texas, until early 1993.[37]

The National Firearms Act establishes a fairly comprehensive tax and registration system governing the manufacture, transfer, and possession of certain firearms including, especially, "machineguns."[38] The federal Criminal Code prohibits the "transfer or possession of machineguns" unless they were lawfully registered before 19 May 1986.[39] What that means is the only "machinegun" (automatic weapon) the average American citizen has been allowed to own, by law, since May 1986 is one which was lawfully registered before that time.[40] That also means anyone attempting to purchase automatic weapons before May 1986 could only do so lawfully by registering the weapons with the federal government.[41] All other automatic weapons are illegal.

To Seal, and others involved in weapons smuggling, what made the business risky was that the registration law applied not only to the purchase and transportation of automatic weapons, but also to the kits used to convert semiautomatic into automatic weapons. The type of conversion kit, or CAR, that has been most widely used for the Colt AR-15 rifle is the M-16 E-2.[42] Various parts for such kits were being manufactured at several small plants and machine shops in Arkansas in the early-to-mid-1980s, including Iver Johnson's and Brodix, all of which was perfectly legal at the time.

However, another federal law, the Boland Amendment, came into play where the Contras were concerned. The Boland Amendment was one of those federal laws the CIA held in particular disdain. It prohibited the exportation of arms like M-16s and kits, like the CARs used to convert semiautomatic weapons, without congressional approval. In the 1980s, the Reagan administration was well aware of the fact that the chances of obtaining congressional approval for such covert CIA activities as arming military and paramilitary groups, like the freedom fighters, were slim to none. Reagan and the CIA also understood the threat posed by the existence of another Communist regime in Latin America, to American interests in that area and to the interests of democracy in general.

Operation Centaur Rose was the name of the CIA gun-running project Seal was involved in, according to Reed and Cummings.[43] Seal is credited with having made approximately three flights per week between 1983 and 1986, from Mena and Nella (another Arkansas hamlet with an airstrip, a few miles from Mena) to Central and South America. On each trip Seal, and until his death in 1985, Emile Camp would haul crates of weapons, CARs, miscellaneous weapons parts, and ammunition to some prearranged location, usually in Nicaragua or Panama, unload the armaments, and either pick up a load of drugs or head for Colombia to do so. At times, some of the big-ticket items obtained through the insurance loss claim scam were also transported in The Fat Lady. At the same time, incredible amounts of cash were transported to and from Latin America, representing payment for drugs, arms, and equipment.[44]

Seal's exploits as a soldier of fortune made him a very wealthy man. But, they also made him a marked man. As long as the Agency got any monies it was entitled to, some CIA agents involved in Centaur Rose were apparently not concerned about the other things Seal transported from Latin America, including cocaine, marijuana, and heroin. Between 1980 and 1986, Seal is believed to have smuggled at least 36 metric tons of cocaine, 104 tons of marijuana, and 3 tons of heroin into Arkansas alone. It is also documented that at the time of his death in February 1986, Seal had several sizeable accounts in BCCI-affiliated banks, including a branch of the Fuji Bank in the Cayman Islands. According to Ambrose Evans-Pritchard, an investigative reporter for a London newspaper, one interest-bearing account opened by Seal at the Fuji Bank in the Caymans had a balance of $1.645 billion at the time one of his articles was written in 1994.[45]

Former Arkansas State Police Investigator Russell Welch has been quoted as saying he believed Arkansas was a main thoroughfare into which most of the flow of drugs from Central America entered the United States in the 1980s. In Welch's words, "Now we know that there were hundreds of millions of dollars worth of cocaine coming into the small state of Arkansas [in the 1980s]."[46]

By 1984, Barry Seal found himself in a "catch-22." The DEA, long aware of his drug-smuggling activities, had finally caught up with him in Florida, where federal prosecutors had a field day. Seal was convicted on numerous charges. Soon, federal prosecutors in Louisiana were breathing down his neck. After his trip to Washington where he met with the Vice-Presidential Task Force, Seal had become the DEA's prize informant. The problem, for Seal anyway, was that, during this entire period, government agents at various levels were working independently of each other to hit the same target. That target was the Medellin cartel.

The fact that Seal had cut a deal with the DEA in exchange for DEA assistance in his federal prosecution in Louisiana, was apparently never convéyed to the CIA. It also appears that the DEA in Louisiana was not contacted by the DEA in Florida, regarding Seal's status as an informant, until it was too late. Moreover, state agencies, like the Arkansas State Police Criminal Investigation Division, and federal agencies, including U.S. Customs, the FBI, and the Criminal Investigation Division (CID) of the IRS, were investigating Seal's operations in Arkansas and elsewhere, apparently independent of each other for the most part.[47] It may well be that the CIA was hesitant to divulge Seal's activities on its behalf for fear that a leak would jeopardize its effectiveness in aiding the Contras. Likewise, the DEA in Florida may have been concerned about losing its key informant if information about Seal's DEA-related activities was conveyed to anyone else. It isn't every day that one of the top five drug smugglers in the country turns informant. At any rate, by 1986 Barry Seal found himself wearing three very uncomfortable hats; those of key man, straw man, and scapegoat.

The Last Sting

In February 1986, Barry Seal was preparing to be the government's chief witness in the pending trial of Colombian drug-lord Jorge Luis Ochoa Vasquez, head of the notorious Ochoa family of the Medellin cartel. According to the DEA, Ochoa was "the world's largest cocaine dealer."[48] At the time, he was in custody in Spain, fighting extradition to Florida.

Seal and Ochoa had been doing business for years. The pot-bellied daredevil once boasted that he could make $1.5 million in a matter of hours dealing with Ochoa as long as he had his pocket pager, two payphones to call Colombia and Miami, and fuel for The Fat Lady.[49] But, since 1984, Seal's luck had been running out. That was the year Seal was first convicted on major drug-trafficking charges in Florida. It was also the year certain authorities in Arkansas began investigating the Mena operation.

Edward Jay Epstein, writing in the *Wall Street Journal* in 1994, said the increased level of activity at the Mena complex in 1984 led to its investigation by certain individuals with the Arkansas State Police CID. Special Agent Russell Welch was particularly interested in the increase in cash transactions in local banks. He was well aware of the drug-smuggling activity and logically concluded it was creating a problem that only a money-laundering scheme of gargantuan proportions could ameliorate.

Soon, IRS CID Special Agent William Duncan was asking questions; and Barry Seal was perhaps the one man on earth who could answer those questions. Even though his testimony was critical to the government's case against Ochoa, as one writer has suggested, Seal knew far more about drug trafficking in Arkansas, and "where the bodies were buried," than he knew about Colombia, and he could have helped put a number of prominent American politicians and officials behind bars.[50]

As Seal sat in his car in the parking lot of a Baton Rouge halfway house on that cold overcast day in February 1986, he must've suspected he was in an extremely vulnerable position. The CIA was protecting its turf. The DEA was doing the same. The FBI and IRS were pulling up the rear, and at least one special agent with the Arkansas State Police CID was scratching around for information. And, because of Judge Frank Polozola's gross negligence in forcing Seal to adjust his lifestyle to fit into an orderly and completely predictable routine, everyone knew exactly where Barry Seal would be after 5:00 P.M. each day.

Who really hired Vasquez, Quintero-Cruz, and Velez to assassinate America's number one drug informant? Was it Ochoa? Was it Escobar? Was it Noreiga? Why not the CIA? One thing is for sure: Barry Seal was never able to testify against any of them. He was never able to testify against William Jefferson Blythe Clinton either.

Endnotes

1. Much of the factual information about Seal is based on the author's personal knowledge. He grew up three blocks from the Seal family, in the same neighborhood in Baton Rouge, Louisiana. The author's oldest brother knew Seal in high school. Both learned to fly from the same Civil Air Patrol instructor at the same private airport. Some of the facts related to Seal's death are also based on the author's

personal knowledge; the rest were gleaned from articles in the *New Orleans Times Picayune* and *States Item*, published between November 1985 and May 1986. Some of the facts regarding the trial of Seal's killers are from the *Baton Rouge Morning Advocate* and *State Times*, in addition to the New Orleans papers. Where necessary, the stories are specifically referred to.

2. From official records of the death of Adler Berriman Seal, on file with the Baton Rouge, Louisiana, City Police, 21 February 1986.

3. Terry Reed and John Cummings, *Compromised* (NY: S.P.I. Books, 1994), 58.

4. Seal and the others were arrested for alleged violations of the Mutual Security Act of 1954, a federal law barring the exportation of explosives without prior State Department approval. Seal's airplane, with a cargo of some thirteen thousand pounds of C-4 explosives, was seized in Louisiana in 1972. Ibid.

5. In his cross-examination, in the trial of *United States v. Norman Saunders*, et al., Cr. no. 85-165-Spellman, United States District Court, Southern District of Florida, in September 1985, Seal testified that the DEA allowed him to make six hundred thousand dollars to seven hundred thousand dollars from drug-smuggling while acting as an informant. The DEA called the money "trafficker funds." The DEA also allowed Seal to pay Emile Camp and other pilots like Roger Reeves, out of the trafficker funds. See, transcript of Seal's cross-examination, pp. 506-508. The Saunders case was consolidated with criminal actions against Stafford Missick, Aulden Smith, and Andre' Fournier, and tried before Judge John H. Moore, II, and a jury, in September 1985.

6. Bustamonte was ultimately prosecuted by the U.S. attorney in Miami, along with Pablo Escobar, Carlos Lehder, Felix Dixon Bates, and Rodriguez Garcia. See, Barry Seal's cross-examination in *United States v. Norman Saunders*, et al., Cr. no. 85-165-Spellman, United States District Court, Southern District of Florida, September 1985.

7. *New Orleans Times Picayune*, 6 March 1986, reported that Seal's brother, Ben (also known as "Benjy"), had commented that there was nothing Barry Seal couldn't fly. "He never had a lesson on a helicopter, he just took one up one day after watching a few times."

8. Ibid.

9. The criminal case against Seal was entitled, *United States of America v. Adler Berriman Seal*, criminal docket number 84-77, section B, United States District Court, Middle District of Louisiana.

10. *Times Picayune*, 6 March 1986.

11. From the official record in *United States of America v. Adler Berriman Seal*.

12. According to a story by Ambrose Evans-Pritchard, in the 9 October 1994, issue of the *London Sunday Telegraph*, one interest-bearing account opened by Seal in the Cayman Islands had a balance of over $1.6 billion at the time the article was written.

13. See, transcript of cross-examination of Adler Berriman Seal, in *United States v. Norman Saunders*, et al., Cr. no. 85-165-Spellman, U.S. District Court, Southern District of Florida, pp. 340, 341. See, also, "Government's Response to Defendant's Rule 32 Motion to Correct Pre-Sentence Report," *United States of America v. Adler Berriman Seal*, Crim. no. 84-77-B, U.S. District Court, Middle District of Louisiana, filed 21 January 1986.

14. Transcript of Barry Seal's cross-examination in September 1985, in *United States v. Norman Saunders*, et al., Cr. no. 85-165-Spellman, U.S. District Court, Southern District of Florida, p. 462.

15. Ibid., 357, 377.

16. Ibid.; see, also, *New Orleans Times Picayune*, 6 March 1986.

17. From transcript of Seal's cross-examination, *U.S. v. Saunders*, et al., pp. 517-520.

18. Ibid., 484-495.

19. Ibid., 521-531.

20. Ibid., 542-557.

21. Ibid., 573-575.

22. Ibid., 521; Reed and Cummings, *Compromised*, 221, 223.

23. From transcript of Seal's cross-examination, *U.S. v. Saunders*, et al., pp. 584-585.

24. "ABC News," in association with Kuhnhart Productions, put together a documentary a few years ago entitled "The Informers," about federally protected witnesses. Several clips from "Uncle Sam Wants You," were included in the film, which has been aired on cable television networks in recent years.

25. "Motion to Correct Sentence and to Enforce Plea Agreement," filed in *U.S. v. Seal*, Crim. no. 84-77-B, U.S. District Court, Middle District of Louisiana, filed 30 December 1985 (emphasis added).

26. Letter of 19 November 1985, prepared by U.S. Attorney Stanford O. Bardwell, on file of record in *U.S. v. Seal*, Crim. no. 84-77-B, U.S. District Court, Middle District of Louisiana.

27. *U.S. v. Seal*.

28. Seal's lawyer wrote the U.S. Probation Office on 18 February 1986. A copy of the letter is in the Court's record, in *U.S. v. Seal*.

29. Minute entry, 8 January 1986, *U.S. v. Seal*.

30. See, transcript of Seal's cross-examination in *U.S. v. Saunders*, et al.

31. Despite the fact that the parts of the Reed and Cummings book, *Compromised*, which are obviously written by Reed, contain mostly flattering autobiographical hyperbole, often about his exploits in Southeast Asia during the Vietnam conflict (he carefully avoids references to Vietnam itself, never having set foot on Vietnamese soil), a few of Reed's statements about Seal and the CIA seem fairly accurate, if for no other reason than having been confirmed by other, more reliable sources.

32. Reed and Cummings, *Compromised*, 43.

33. Ibid.

34. Ibid., 50.

35. Ibid., 50-54.

36. Ibid.

37. "Official Report of the Department of the Treasury on the Bureau of Alcohol, Tobacco, and Firearms Investigation of Vernon Wayne Howell," also known as "David Koresh," September 1993.

38. See, Title 26 U.S. Code, chapter 53, section 5845(b).

39. Title 18, U.S. Code, section 922(o).

40. Qualified Americans could, until recently, apply for and receive a license to sell automatic weapons and conversion kits.

41. Since May 1986, the law has flatly prohibited the transfer or possession of automatic weapons not registered before the May 1986 cut-off date.

42. The CAR kit includes a complete upper rear and barrel assembly, buttstock, recoil spring and buffer, M-16 hammer, trigger, disconnector, selector, M-16 auto sear, pins, springs, trigger guard, magazine release, and bolt hold-open. See, "Report of the Department of the Treasury on the Bureau of Alcohol, Tobacco, and Firearms Investigation of Vernon Wayne Howell," September 1993.

43. Reed and Cummings, *Compromised*, 108.

44. Ibid., 144.

45. Ambrose Evans-Pritchard, *London Sunday Telegraph*, 9 October 1994.

46. Matrisciana, *Clinton Chronicles*, 51.

47. Reed and Cummings, *Compromised*, 106-108.

48. *New Orleans Times Picayune*, 21 February 1986.

49. Ibid., 6 March 1986.

50. Patrick Matrisciana, *The Clinton Chronicles Book* (Hemet, CA: Jeremiah Books, 1994).

Chapter Five

BCCI,
The Big Money Laundry

Like the Knights Templar of the fourteenth century, who started a banking empire based as much on their desire to fund crusading warriors as to line their own pockets, the men who started the Bank of Credit and Commerce International also had a business philosophy rooted and grounded in religion and theology. That religion was Islam.

In October 1988, BCCI and eight of its key employees were indicted in federal court in Tampa, Florida, as a result of DEA undercover efforts in a project known as Operation C-Chase. In November 1990, three of those indicted, Khalid Awan, Akbar Bilgrami, and Syed Aftab Hussain, were sentenced to federal prison for laundering millions of dollars for Colombia's Medellin cartel.[1] But, if that was the beginning of BCCI's sorrows, it would soon be eclipsed by the actions of the British government.

On 5 July 1991, the Bank of England completely shut down BCCI's twenty-five branches in Great Britain.

The same thing happened almost simultaneously in the United States, France, the Cayman Islands, Spain, and Switzerland, but BCCI's London operations were by far the most important to its worldwide system. According to Robin Leigh-Pemberton, then-governor of the Bank of England, BCCI was engaging in "fraudulent conduct on a worldwide scale." At the time, on paper at least, BCCI had $208 billion in assets in four hundred branches in seventy-three countries. The ubiquitous banking conglomerate employed over fourteen thousand people in 1991.[2]

Prior to its downfall in the early 1990s, BCCI was arguably the most powerful financial organization on earth. That enormous success can be attributed, in large part, to a vast network of political connections reaching from centers of finance and power like London, New York, and Washington to obscure places like Envigado, Colombia (the hometown of drug lord Pablo Escobar), the Cayman Islands, and even Arkansas. BCCI was a "king" maker in every sense of the word. And, understanding something about the history and background of BCCI is critical to understanding the global politics of drugs, oil, and arms smuggling that ultimately brought one of those kings, Bill Clinton, to power.

The Arab Imperialists

King Faisal acceded to the Saudi Arabian throne in 1964. A foe of U.S. protectionism toward Israel, he sent Sheik Yamani to Washington, D.C., in April 1973 to warn President Nixon that unless Israel could be persuaded to quit the occupied territory, including Jerusalem (which had been captured in the June 1967 war), the Saudis would reduce their oil production levels.[3]

After a meeting with Egyptian President Anwar Sadat on 23 August 1973, Faisal stated publicly that "America's complete support of Zionism against the Arabs makes it extremely difficult for us to continue to support the U.S. petroleum needs."[4]

On Yom Kippur (the Day of Atonement) during the first week in October 1973, Egyptian and Syrian military forces assaulted Israeli forces on the Golan Heights and in northern Israel. After waffling for a couple of weeks, on October 20 Nixon thumbed his nose at Faisal and resupplied Israel's army. As a result, the price of OPEC oil shot up from three dollars per thirty-three-gallon barrel to over twelve dollars for the same barrel practically overnight. Since that time, the price has increased on a fairly regular basis.[5]

King Faisal's hatred of Israel was well known. He routinely presented his visitors with copies of the *Protocols of the Meetings of the Learned Elders of Zion,* an extremely anti-Semitic book that's generally recognized as a forgery.[6] In spite of the clearly fraudulent nature of the *Protocols,* Faisal and others of the Moslem faith believe them to be principles by which most powerful Jewish business and political leaders live. Disseminating copies of the inflammatory book helped them kindle the flames of anti-Semitism in the Middle East.[7]

By 1975, Faisal was still preaching against the evils of Zionism, but his tactics had changed. Arab ownership of American businesses was growing at an unprecedented rate, and American firms taking advantage of Saudi opportunities were well rewarded. This was especially true of Sun-Belt firms which were feeling the brunt of an oil-induced recession at the time. For example, CRS Design Associates, a Houston architectural firm, increased its employment from 250 in 1976 to 700 in 1977. That growth was based mainly on Saudi projects. By 1977, fully half of CRS's $35 million in gross revenues came from the Middle East. In 1978, Saudi financier Ghaith Pharaon bought 20 percent of CRS for $5.5 million.[8]

During this same time frame, American business interests were borrowing millions from Arab banks and the Saudi Monetary Agency. Chrysler Corporation borrowed a total of $100 million from eighteen separate Arab banks; and AT&T and U.S. Steel Corporation borrowed $650 million and $200 million, respectively, from the Saudi Monetary Agency.[9]

Petrodollars also bought instant political gratitude, especially in small states like Arkansas. In December 1975, relatives of Rose Law Firm attorney Webb Hubbell's wife, Suzanna Ward Hubbell, found themselves on the receiving end of a fat Saudi contract. That month, Ward Industries of Conway, Arkansas, which manufactured school buses, received a $20 million order for seven hundred specially designed school buses, to be shipped to Saudi Arabia to shuttle Muslim pilgrims to Mecca. The impact of this contract on the Ward family and on Conway, a town of 15,510 people in central Arkansas, was profound. When this contract was followed by a $60 million order from an Egyptian company, Ward had to hire three hundred new employees for its assembly line. The order accounted for 25 percent of Ward's production that year. By mid-1977, Ward had firmed up plans for an assembly plant in Jidda, Saudi Arabia, as part of a joint venture with Saudi businessman Ghaith Pharaon.[10]

U.S. Sen. J. William Fulbright, an Arkansas Democrat and an outspoken Xenophobe, was chairman of the Senate Foreign Relations Committee in the early seventies, where he helped Frederick G. Dutton, a Washington lawyer and long-time Democrat, build coalitions between the Saudis and American business concerns interested in establishing ties with the Saudis. When Fulbright lost his bid for a sixth term in 1974, his thirty-two-year congressional career was over, but he quickly established a new one through his Washington law firm, Hogan & Hartson, becoming an ambassador of goodwill and a lobbyist for the Arabs.[11]

Another Arkansas Democrat, Sen. Dale Bumpers, was lobbied heavily by business interests in 1981 to support the sale of high-tech command-and-control radar systems, known as AWACs (Advanced Warning and Command systems), to the Saudis. Brown & Root, a very large international engineering and construction firm with significant political clout not only because of the money it sent to campaigns, but also because of its substantial labor force, sent position papers on the AWACs legislation to both Arkansas senators, as did Riceland Foods of Arkansas.[12]

If the Arabs found support from certain segments of the Western business community, they found even stronger—albeit different—support from academia. Often exerting indirect influence over academic organizations, like the Georgetown University Center for Strategic and International Studies, by throwing their weight around with oil companies funding those organizations, the Arabs were described in glowing terms in reports and studies prepared by such groups.

In other cases, the Saudis exerted direct influence. The Atlanta-based Southern Center for International Studies, chaired by Bert Lance, was one of the first recipients of Arab money, through the West Foundation, named for one-time South Carolina Gov. John C. West. In September 1979, Duke University president Terry Sanford hosted a university-sponsored conference which, in part, extolled the virtues of doing business with the Saudis. In 1984, he travelled to the Middle East to meet with business, educational, and political leaders from the region. In October of that year, Sanford hosted a dinner in honor of Saudi businessman Ghaith Pharaon, who had been developing a golf course in the Richmond Hill section of Savannah, Georgia. Pharaon had close ties to Jimmy Carter at the time and supported Carter's visionary Global 2000. One oil company, Aramco, alone disbursed over $5 million to lobbyists, academicians, and educational institutions and trusts to give Americans a better impression of the Arab world.[13]

Algerian oil interests retained Clark Clifford, the quintessential Democratic party bellwether, who had come to Washington from St. Louis in 1945 as a congressional aide and who had served in the administrations of Harry S. Truman, John F. Kennedy, and Lyndon

Johnson. Clifford had been Kennedy's personal attorney
and Johnson's secretary of defense. His law firm, Clifford
& Warnke, represented presidents, bureaucrats, and
Fortune 500 companies like TWA, Dupont, and AT&T.
Clifford had strongly supported U.S. recognition of Israel as a state when serving as special counsel to President Truman, but he apparently didn't feel he was taking an inconsistent position or being hypocritical by
acting as a paid emissary for Israel's enemies twenty-five
years later. From 1970 to 1977, Clifford's law firm received over $1 million in fees from Algeria alone for
legal services and expenses.[14]

With the ever-increasing influence of Arab oil money
in the West in the mid-1970s, due in large part to the
efforts of men like Clark Clifford, came a growing desire
on the part of Arab investors to gain positions of strength
in the American banking industry. But, because of nearly
three decades of Democratic party control over Congress, during which time protectionism had become the
hallmark of American economic policy, our banking laws
were not very accommodating to foreign investors. For
that reason, men like Agha Hasan Abedi, founder of
BCCI, had to use stealth tactics to accomplish their goals.

Financial General Bankshares, Inc., a holding company that owned thirteen banks with 150 branches in
New York, the District of Columbia, Virginia, Maryland,
Tennessee, and Georgia, was taken over in the 1970s by
three Arab investors: Kamal Adham (chief of Saudi
Arabian Intelligence); Faisal Saud al-Fulaij (chairman of
Kuwait Airways); and Crown Prince Mohammed of the
United Arab Emerites. At the time, Financial General
had assets of over $2.2 billion and was one of only a
handful of banks allowed to engage in interstate banking. One of the banks it controlled was the Atlanta-based
National Bank of Georgia.[15] Clark Clifford was made
chairman of Financial General's board of directors soon
after the takeover was completed. When the papers were

signed and the dust finally settled, BCCI had somehow gotten its foot in the door and was on its way to becoming a major force to be reckoned with in the American banking community.[16]

The Islamic Bank

Estimates of the profits from cocaine sales in the U.S. reach as high as $110 billion a year. Massive profits are also gleaned from the arms-smuggling trade. During the 1980s and into the early 1990s, BCCI was the place to launder those profits. The bank's list of customers read like a Who's Who of clandestine operations around the globe. From Shakar Farhan, who was later discovered to be none other than the notorious Palestinian terrorist, Abu Nidal, to corrupt public officials, illegal drug and arms merchants, and even the CIA, the "secret account" was a BCCI specialty. Abu Nidal's Fatah Revolutionary Council kept an average of $60 million in one such account at BCCI's Sloane Street branch in London. The money was used to finance terrorism and arms-smuggling operations worldwide.[17] Some of those weapons ended up in Nicaragua, in the hands of the Freedom Fighters. They got there by way of Arkansas.

BCCI was chartered in Luxemburg in 1972 by Agha Hasan Abedi after years of hard work, attention to detail, and careful planning. Abedi was born in India in 1922. Like 80 million other Muslims living like exiles in predominantly Hindu India, Abedi moved to Pakistan when it officially became a nation in 1947. A Shiite Muslim, Hasan Abedi had grown up believing he was destined for fame and fortune. He earned a law degree at an Indian university, but, because of his social status, he was only able to land a job as a teller at the Habib Bank in Bombay. It was there that Abedi began forming his banking philosophy. He dreamed of having his own bank someday, whose policies regarding loans, interest rates, and investments would be based on Islamic concepts of power, patronage, and piety. Abedi wanted to present the image that BCCI would be a Third World bank.[18]

Hasan Abedi was always eager to meet anyone who might put him in touch with a would-be depositor or investor, and he catered to those types of people. In 1966, he began cultivating a relationship with Sheik Zayed bin Sultan al-Nahayan of Abu Dhabi. Although Abedi was most interested in landing the sheik as a client, he recognized that arranging outings, such as falcon hunts, and other recreational activities for the sheik, would eventually pay off. The plan worked, and soon Abedi found himself being introduced to members of the royal families of Oman, Kuwait, Qatar, Bahrain, and the United Arab Emerites.[19]

In 1972, Abedi flew to New York to discuss the BCCI idea with Roy P.M. Carlson, an executive with the Bank of America in San Francisco. After hearing Abedi's plan for a bank capitalized with Arab oil money, catering to the financial needs of the more progressive Third World countries, and helping fund humanitarian projects on a global scale, Carlson was interested. And, if Carlson was interested, Bank of America was interested.

The Middle East was also a very dynamic region in 1972 in terms of both cultural and economic change. The formation of OPEC, and threats of unilateral oil production freezes and price increases, had more than a few eyes looking nervously in that direction. Bank of America wanted an entree into Middle Eastern banking, and Carlson believed Abedi could help make that dream a reality.[20]

Before Abedi and Carlson parted company, they formulated a plan for BCCI. For 25 percent of the stock, Bank of America would invest $2.5 million. Abedi could then take an investment proposal to the Persian Gulf rulers he had met through Sheik Zayed, showing them that the world's largest bank (Bank of America) already had a 25 percent interest in the venture. Two prominent Arabs committed almost immediately: Kamal Adham and Faisal Saud al-Fulaij. In a matter of weeks, BCCI was formally chartered in Luxemburg, a country whose banking laws are as friendly to the banking industry as Delaware's corporate laws are to American business concerns. Abedi had control over BCCI's day-to-day operations, and Bank of America was able to place two members on the BCCI board.[21]

When OPEC choked off the flow of Middle Eastern oil in 1973, inflating prices over 400 percent overnight, money began flowing into the Persian Gulf region faster than anyone could have imagined. BCCI's growth exceeded that of the oil industry, and during that year it opened branches in the Kensington High Street, Sloane Street, and Knightsbridge sections of London, where there is a large Arab population. With this phenomenal growth came phenomenal managerial problems. While BCCI abhorred the strict scrutiny of the bank examiners in London, it otherwise found British banking laws to its liking. For that reason, BCCI registered in the Cayman Islands in 1975 as a subsidiary of BCCI Holdings SA. With management operations in two places, separated by a rather large ocean, BCCI felt more comfortable and was open to new, more diverse opportunities.[22]

Thomas Bertram "Bert" Lance had a background similar to that of Hasan Abedi. Like Abedi, Lance's first position in banking was as a teller. And, like Abedi, Lance had learned the value of being properly "connected." Among Lance's connections was Georgia Gov. Jimmy Carter. In fact, when Carter ran for president, Lance ran for governor of Georgia. The only problem was that Lance had family ties to the First National Bank of Calhoun and sloppily overdrew his campaign checking account on numerous occasions. He didn't get elected, but he did become president of the National Bank of Georgia (NBG) at the bank's behest. Lance's sole precondition for serving as president was that the bank allow him to buy a sizeable block of its stock. That block, of 120,000 shares, was sold to Lance in 1975 by Financial General Bankshares, Inc., the holding company which controlled NBG, at a cost of $2.6 million. Lance borrowed the money to buy the stock from Manufacturers Hanover Trust of New York.[23]

In 1976, President Carter named Lance director of the Office of Management and Budget (OMB). OMB oversees the financial affairs of the executive branch of government and prepares the official federal budget. Things did not go smoothly with Lance's appointment. Among his looming problems were that Manufacturers Hanover had placed its own precondition on Lance's stock loan; he was to remain president of NBG until the loan was paid off. But, as fate would have it, federal regulations prohibited the director of OMB from also being an officer in a financial institution doing business with the public. Then, the value of NBG stock took a nose dive, and Lance didn't have the funds to both take the loss on the stock sale and repay the loan. He also owed eight hundred thousand dollars to Chemical Bank of New York. Bert Lance needed nearly $3.5 million to retire the principal amounts due the two banks. Unable to sell his NBG stock to cover these obligations, Lance's alternative was to borrow $3.4 million. Lance's financial problems would eventually help Abedi accomplish some of his goals for BCCI.[24]

During this same period of time, George Olmsted, then-chairman of NBG, met with Lance and William Middendorf II, who had served as secretary of the navy under both Nixon and Ford and was a Financial General stockholder. Olmsted asked Lance to consider buying control of Financial General, but Lance declined. A couple of months later, in early 1977, a group of investors led by Middendorf was attempting a leveraged buyout of Financial General when a schism occurred because of the way one of the investor's agents was treated by Middendorf. That investor was Jackson Stephens, Jimmy Carter's roommate at the United States Naval Academy and president and CEO of Stephens, Inc., of Little Rock, the largest investment brokerage west of Wall Street. Stephens then led his own faction of investors in a search for a buyer to force Middendorf to sell his interest in Financial General. Eugene Metzger, a member of the Stephens faction, suggested that a foreign bank might be interested in buying the company. That bank was BCCI.[25]

Before the news that Bert Lance needed to sell his NBG stock hit the street, Hasan Abedi was behind the scenes already taking steps toward making the acquisition a reality, not by BCCI directly, but rather, indirectly through loans to trusted BCCI customers. Abedi had befriended Lance, Jimmy Carter, Jackson Stephens, and Clark Clifford, and learned during a meeting at Stephens' office about Lance's situation long before it was reported by the media. Abedi probably salivated when he considered the prospect of controlling Financial General, with its 150 branches in thirteen states, but BCCI couldn't be directly involved in any stock purchases because of Bank of America's ownership interest, which had increased from 25 percent, at the time BCCI was originally chartered in 1972 to over 40 percent in 1977.[26]

Abedi's other option was indirect ownership by offering to help Lance find a buyer for his NBG stock in exchange for Lance's help in finding a suitable investment for BCCI. The NBG buyer would be Ghaith Pharaon, the man who was in the process of forming a joint venture with relatives of Webb Hubbell's wife in the construction of an assembly plant in Saudi Arabia. [27]

Ghaith Pharaon, of Syrian descent but Saudi-born, was educated at the Colorado School of Mines and then earned an M.B.A. from Harvard. When he returned home, he served for a while in Sheik Ahmad Zaki Yamani's oil ministry. Later on, he formed Saudi Re-

search & Development Corporation, earning a small
fortune from his first entrepreneurial endeavor. However, Pharaon wasn't particularly happy in the Middle
East and soon began looking for investment opportunities in the West.

In 1974, Pharaon found one of those opportunities,
buying one million shares of stock in Occidental Petroleum, Armand Hammer's company. The next year,
Pharaon bought Bank of Commonwealth, a Detroit bank
which had been placed in receivership to the Federal
Deposit Insurance Corporation three years earlier. A
year later, he broke even on the sale of his Commonwealth stock. In early 1977, Pharaon bought 20 percent
of Main Bank in Houston, which he sold at a substantial
profit later that year just as he was hearing that Bert
Lance's huge block of stock in NBG was for sale. In
March 1977, he joined Adham, al-Fulaij, and Abdullah
Darwaish in forming Kuwait International Finance Company, which bought a 16 percent interest in Attock Petroleum, an old, well-established British company.[28]

When Hasan Abedi flew to Little Rock in early 1977
to meet with Lance and Jackson Stephens, he was hop-
ing that somehow, as a result of that consultation, BCCI
would end up with a firm ownership interest in an American bank. Stephens dominated the conversation by blow-
ing sales puff in Abedi's direction about Financial General. Impressed that Financial General might be BCCI's
ticket into the American market—the investment he had
hoped to find with Bert Lance's help—Abedi quickly
arranged for Kamal Adham, the former chief of Saudi
intelligence and a major stockholder in BCCI, to begin
buying blocks of stock in Financial General. At the same
time, he sent Swaleh Naqvi, second in command at BCCI,
to London to get $1.35 million from BCCI for Adham's
first stock purchase. The trick for BCCI would be to buy
blocks of stock, each representing 4.9 percent or less of
the total outstanding shares of Financial General, to avoid

the scrutiny of the Securities and Exchange Commission. Abedi's next step was to hire Clark Clifford and his law firm, Clifford & Warnke, to do the legal work for the takeover.[29]

One advantage the Financial General deal had over others considered by Abedi was that a grandfather clause, in a 1956 law which otherwise precluded holding companies from controlling banks in more than one state, made an exception for Financial General. As a result, it controlled thirteen banks in five states and the District of Columbia. The Arab investors who, after lengthy litigation, would ultimately wind up with nearly 75 percent of the outstanding stock in Financial General, using BCCI money, were Kamal Adham, Faisal Saud al- Fulaij, Crown Prince Mohammed, and Abdullah Darwaish. Adham and al-Fulaij were also major BCCI stockholders.[30]

In 1978, Abedi formed Credit and Commerce American Holdings (CCAH) in the Netherland Antilles to facilitate the buyout of Financial General. In October of that year, CCAH applied with the Federal Reserve for approval of the Financial General acquisition. Banking officials from a couple of the states in which Financial General was doing business objected to the new acquisition as a hostile takeover, and in February 1979, the Federal Reserve Board dismissed the Arab group's application. An appeal ensued, but while it was pending in July 1980, the group offered $130 million and promised that the Arabs—Adham, al-Fulaij, and Darwaish (who would each wind up with 24 percent of the outstanding stock in the company)—would play only a passive role in the day-to-day operations and management of Financial General. Ultimate decision-making authority would be placed in the hands of a board of directors, not the three Arab stockholders whose combined interests would be more than enough to control the bank.[31]

In a very complicated scheme, Banque Arabe et Internationale Investissement of Paris was involved in the Arab takeover of Financial General, as was International Credit and Investment Company Overseas, a partially employee-owned subsidiary of BCCI, and BCCI's main branch in the Cayman Islands. Kamal Adham first deposited $30 million in Banque Arabe, as collateral for a $50 million loan. This $30 million represented the proceeds of a $30 million signature loan to Adham and Faisal Saud al-Fulaij from International Credit, which the two Arabs would use to buy their shares of Financial General. In another typical BCCI shell game, a series of secret side agreements made the deal a reality.

First, a secret agreement between International Credit and Adham provided that Adham was not even liable to International Credit on the $30 million credit. A second agreement provided that neither Adham nor al-Fulaij would be liable to Banque Arabe. BCCI had secretly agreed to repay the Banque Arabe loan. BCCI would "cover" the money loaned by International Credit. Had the Federal Reserve known about these agreements, it never would have approved the takeover. While such agreements may be valid under normal circumstances, federal law clearly provides that they are invalid in the event of the failure of a financial institution (which is normally followed by receivership and final administration by the Resolution Trust Corporation). Those laws, of necessity, enter into the equation when the Federal Reserve is being asked to approve an application for a bank takeover.[32]

Final approval of the Financial General takeover required investigations of the transaction by the SEC, FBI, and CIA. Those enforcement agencies certainly knew about the ties between CCAH, Banque Arabe, and International Credit, but their reports never reflected the incestuous connections. The reports also failed to mention that Kamal Adham had once been the chief of Saudi intelligence. The CIA, in particular, was very familiar with Adham and his former position as head of the Saudi spy network. But then, the CIA also used secret accounts at BCCI in the 1980s for funding its subversive activities worldwide. There is absolutely no doubt that the CIA had knowledge of these covert connections when it filed its report to the Federal Reserve. At any rate, the takeover was finally completed in April 1982, and the name of the bank was changed to First American. In addition to the enormous legal fees pocketed by Clifford & Warnke, Clark Clifford was rewarded for his efforts by being named chairman of First American's first board of directors. In one year in the 1980s, Clifford & Warnke was paid $4 million in legal fees, costs, and expenses by BCCI.[33]

Bert Lance was finally confirmed as Carter's OMB director but couldn't fulfill his promise to resign from National Bank of Georgia and sell his NBG stock because the value of the stock was still too low. Since the meeting in Little Rock at Jackson Stephens' office, Hasan Abedi had been aware of Lance's situation and believed that all Lance needed in order to remain OMB director was sufficient funds to satisfy his obligations to Manufacturer's Hanover and Chemical Bank. By assuring him that BCCI would make the deal work, Abedi urged Ghaith Pharaon to buy Bert Lance's interest in NBG. What happened next was the archetypal BCCI shell game.[34]

In December 1977, Pharaon and Lance reached an agreement in principle which would ultimately result in Pharaon—on paper at least—controlling 60 percent of NBG. The price Pharaon agreed to pay for Lance's stock was $2.4 million (twenty dollars a share). However, Pharaon's purchase was anything but the squeaky-clean, arm's-length transaction it appeared to be. BCCI had made yet another in a long line of under-the-table, signature (unsecured) loans. Viewing the deal objectively, First National Bank of Chicago would fund Lance's bailout by consolidating two obligations into one. The transaction would be executed on 5 January 1978. The only ostensibly strange part of the deal was a side agreement, pursuant to which NBG was to deposit two hundred thousand dollars at First National and move one of its accounts at Continental Illinois Bank to First National. In reality, however, First National received a wire transfer from BCCI Luxemburg in the amount of $3.4 million on 4 January 1978, thus completely retiring Lance's obligation to First National before it even materialized. BCCI carried Lance's credit as a "loan," but it was another of those signature loans, with no specific interest rate, no demand date, no provisions for collection upon default, and no schedule of payments. For Pharaon's part, he hired Roy P.M. Carlson, a veteran of Middle Eastern banking and the man who was responsible for Bank of America originally bank-rolling BCCI, to run NBG. In the final analysis, BCCI had helped Bert Lance remain as OMB director, had helped prominent Saudi businessman Ghaith Pharaon obtain 120,000 shares of NGB, and had helped itself to a rather large piece of the American banking pie.[35]

The World's Largest "Ponzi" Scheme

In 1977, Bank of America owned over 40 percent of BCCI. That same year the first of several Price-Waterhouse accounting audits at BCCI's headquarters branch in London revealed highly questionable loan policies. Of key concern was a lack of security (collateral) for dozens of loans to Arabs. The audit also revealed that most of the correspondence and many of the loan documents were written in Urdu, the native tongue of Pakistan. Consequently, Bank of America decided to sell its interest in BCCI for $34 million.

At that time, Hasan Abedi urged Ghaith Pharaon to buy the BCCI stock owned by Bank of America, assuring him BCCI would be only too happy to do its part in bringing about the sale (as it would do when Pharaon sought the $2.4 million necessary to buy Bert Lance's interest in NBG). In spite of numerous Price-Waterhouse warnings in the 1980s about loan policies that were fast and loose, by 1990, as BCCI was approaching collapse, Pharaon owed a total of $288 million based on signature loans that had never been repaid. Pharaon was just one of many Arabs indebted on paper to BCCI. But, were the obligations legitimate? The answer lies in history—the dark side of history—where frauds and conmen lurk.[36]

In 1919, an Italian immigrant named Ponzi gained fame and fortune in Boston by paying enormous returns on investments through his newly formed company. The longer his customers' money was invested with Ponzi, the greater the return on their investments. The return on a short-term investment was as much as 50 percent, and never less than 25 percent. The return on a six-month or longer investment was as high as 100 percent. The problem for the investors was that Ponzi had no venture capital with which to start his business. Ponzi's venture capital came from his first investor. The investor was playing the role of venture capitalist and didn't know it. An outstanding salesman, cunning confidence man, and convicted forger, Ponzi was able to persuade numerous unsuspecting investors to deposit their life savings in his company's account. Investors weren't hustled en masse, but rather individually, over a period of weeks and months. This allowed Ponzi to pay his initial investors with funds received from later investors. He kept track of the investments in a ledger book and had a tickler system to remind him of who needed to be paid and when the payment was to be made. He made millions in less than a year. However, at some point, an astute reporter for the *Boston Globe* got wind of the enormous returns on investments Ponzi was offering and exposed the scam. Ponzi was convicted of fraud and served time in prison for his scheme.

BCCI's way of doing business was very similar to Charles Ponzi's. Although BCCI had original venture capital (Bank of America had purchased 25 percent of BCCI's outstanding common stock in 1972 at a price of $2.5 million), it didn't retain nearly enough to back the loans it made to its Arab friends over the years, especially on an unsecured basis. Like Ponzi's scheme, initial BCCI investors bought stock and were paid back in the form of loans from BCCI which they were never required to repay. But, these loans were not like dividends. Dividends are paid periodically out of corporate earnings and profits. BCCI didn't pay dividends, it made loans. As a new customer made a deposit, his money was used to provide loans to nominee shareholders, in part to buy interests in American banks. BCCI laundered billion of dollars of drug money in this manner.

For example, in 1983, Panamanian pilot Ricardo Bilonick, who owned an airline specializing in cocaine trafficking for the Medellin cartel, came to BCCI seeking a $1 million loan. He was paying Panamanian strongman, Gen. Manuel Noreiga, to operate in Panama. Noreiga's fees were substantial, but then, so were the profits from the drug trade. Bilonick was initially turned down by BCCI, but a few days later, he heard of a way to finesse a BCCI loan. He just hadn't presented the deal correctly. BCCI expected the borrower to furnish "security" (collateral) in an amount just less than the amount to be borrowed. BCCI would accept this deposit as collateral and would then immediately turn around and loan a little less than the amount deposited to the individual making the deposit. BCCI would get a "loan origination fee," "closing costs," and other miscellaneous items, ultimately netting a respectable sum. In BCCI vernacular, these were "cash collateral advances."[37]

The initial deposit from someone like Ricardo Bilonick, or someone like Barry Seal, was always "black money" (money from the drug trade). BCCI's offshore and Latin American operations didn't have to obey American laws, like the federal Bank Secrecy Act of

1970, which requires the filing of reports in connection with cash transfers of ten thousand dollars or more. All of this made money laundering easy. The BCCI system was conceptually very simple. If a drug dealer brought $1 million in black money to BCCI as collateral for a "loan" of nine hundred thousand dollars and BCCI received one hundred thousand dollars (10 percent) of the amount deposited, for loan origination fees, points, closing costs, and the like, the drug dealer would walk out with loan proceeds of 90 percent of what he had had originally in black money.

Common sense might ask what incentive a drug smuggler could possibly have to exchange $1 million cash for a nine-hundred-thousand-dollar loan. The answer—ignoring for a moment the fact that since the loans were never repaid, no interest had to be paid to BCCI— is that drug smugglers made enormous profits and couldn't get their hands on those profits without incurring laundering costs. A drug trafficker couldn't use black money. It had to be laundered, and it had to be laundered correctly. Barry Seal was clearing $1 million per flight at one time. He was making two, three, and sometimes four flights a week back and forth from Arkansas to Central and South America and the Caribbean. He couldn't enjoy most of that money unless it was properly laundered. Without the BCCI money laundry, smugglers like Bilonick and Seal would have received only a fraction of what they received with the help of BCCI.

In 1989, a special agent with the DEA testified as follows, before the U.S. Senate:

> The Colombian cartels provide drugs to their wholesale distributors which supply the retail distribution network. The money flows from neighborhoods where drugs are sold back to central collection points, generally in cities. The cartels employ specialized money couriers or collectors

who are outside the drug distribution network. These individuals collect, sort, count, and package the money for shipment.[38]

In Miami, Florida, in the late 1970s, the money couriers and collectors the DEA agent referred to were doing a booming business. Banks connected to the drug-trafficking trade were making record currency transactions. The Federal Reserve Bank in Miami had a cash surplus that exceeded the surpluses of all other Federal Reserve Banks combined: $5.5 billion. One BCCI courier, afraid of being robbed because of the huge amounts of cash he was required to carry, was fired by BCCI in 1985. He then went to the IRS with bank records. At first, the IRS approved an undercover investigation by CID agents. But, practically as soon as the project was under way, it was called off by someone in Washington because Miami was just a "small" operation.[39]

Another courier for BCCI's main London branch was uneasy whenever called on to provide transportation for Shakar Farhan. Farhan always had heavy baggage and often carried cases full of cash. In 1985, the courier learned that the bags were heavy because they were full of guns. The courier soon discovered that Farhan was a pseudonym. The man's real name was Abu Nidal, the world's most dreaded terrorist. BCCI had long provided financing for Nidal's organization, the Fatah Revolutionary Council. The council maintained an account in a London branch of BCCI in the amount of $60 million. That same year, BCCI demonstrated its willingness to go above and beyond the call of duty for its customers when it not only provided financing for a large arms shipment for Nidal's use in Syria, but also arranged for an African diplomat to sign phony documents claiming the arms were headed for his country. The subterfuge was necessary because the British government prohibited the sending of arms to Syria.[40]

The first official raid on a BCCI branch in the United

States occurred in the mid-1980s in Chicago. IRS CID agents joined DEA agents in storming the Chicago branch of BCCI for its failure to file CTRs on amounts of ten thousand dollars or more placed on deposit at the bank. That was only the beginning of sorrows for BCCI. In 1986, another Price-Waterhouse audit uncovered a startling revelation: BCCI had lost between $300 million and $500 million due to the churning of deposits in the commodities futures and foreign currency markets. Most of the churning was engineered by lower level personnel responding to orders from Swaleh Naqvi, second in command at BCCI, for more growth and greater profits. Desperate, Abedi leaned on his old friend, Sheik Zayed of Abu Dhabi for capital infusion. Zayed was only able to provide $150 million; the rest would have to come from the sale of BCCI stock. Another $150 million was provided by the Mahfouz family, who owned the National Commercial Bank of Saudi Arabia. Of course, in typical "Ponzi" fashion, BCCI turned around and loaned the Mahfouz brothers $141 million on a completely unsecured basis.[41]

Shortly after the first wave of bad news from Price-Waterhouse hit BCCI, Operation Greenback—a combined effort by the IRS CID and the DEA—got underway. Its purpose was to locate the largest money launderers, gather evidence against them, and get grand jury indictments as quickly as possible. Greenback was responding to a new fad in money laundering called "smurfing." It involved the use of numerous couriers with small amounts of cash, going to as many different launderers as they could find.[42]

In 1986, the DEA began its own money-laundering investigation called Operation C-Chase in Tampa, Florida. It was through C-Chase that the DEA finally gathered enough evidence to bust BCCI. BCCI had twenty offices in Colombia in 1986. Drug smugglers in Tampa could bank directly with the local BCCI office, which would in turn deal directly with a BCCI branch in Colombia. As a service to its preferred customers, BCCI would, upon request, move an account to any BCCI branch in the world in a matter of minutes. The records of the account would follow in a matter of days. The BCCI branch in Panama City was a favorite location for smugglers to move accounts from Colombia.

The Panama City operation was conceptually simple, involving a series of shell corporations. Black money was first deposited into an account at BCCI in the name of a dummy corporation. BCCI would then issue U.S. Treasury checks in approximately the same amount. These checks would be posted at American banks, and when they cleared, the banks would remit to BCCI and the dummy corporation. This scheme continued until the late 1980s when the DEA finally caught up with the top people at the BCCI office in Tampa.[43]

The BCCI-Noreiga Connection

Since 1982, the Medellin cartel had been paying vast sums of money to Panamanian dictator, Gen. Manuel Noreiga, to use Panama as a way station for drug traffickers. Noreiga allowed smugglers to ship cocaine to the U.S. through Panamanian ports and airstrips. He protected their drug labs, gave them a safe haven, and helped them launder money. Steven Kalish, a drug smuggler with a booming business, netted $35 million from marijuana alone in 1983, the year Noreiga came to power. In order to better protect his business interests and insure that he would be welcome in Panama City, he paid Noreiga hundreds of thousands of dollars. In return, Noreiga also helped Kalish open an account at BCCI, where Noreiga had about $20 million in a personal account in the name of the "Panamanian Defense Fund."[44]

On 2 November 1988, federal prosecutors in Miami indicted Noreiga and certain leaders of the Medellin cartel. The Panamanian strong man immediately moved his money offshore to BCCI branches in the Cayman Islands. But, it would not be until December 1990, after the U.S. military sent paratroopers into Panama City, invaded Noreiga's fortress, and captured him, that he would finally be extradited. At the same time, in Tampa, a federal judge was ruling that BCCI had to forfeit $14.8 million. Adding to BCCI's woes, a federal grand jury in Washington, D.C., served the bank with a subpoena for information in connection with the Iran-Contra arms smuggling scandal.[45]

While Noreiga was being extradited to Miami—a situation that was sure to further subject BCCI to the scrutiny of DEA and IRS special investigators—trouble was brewing elsewhere for BCCI. New York County District Attorney Robert Morgenthau and his chief assistant, John Moscow, were hot on the BCCI trail, having been investigating alleged unlawful activities in that area for over a year. Morgenthau and Moscow were convinced that BCCI was operating a Ponzi scheme, but their investigation had been seriously impeded by the U.S. Department of Justice, and in particular, the U.S. attorney's office, as Morgenthau would later testify.

In London, Robin Leigh-Pemberton had received a copy of a Price-Waterhouse audit reflecting insider loans, mainly to CCAH, totaling $856 million. According to the same audit, BCCI had assets of about half that. Swaleh Naqvi immediately began shredding BCCI loan documents and account files around the clock. Further investigation nonetheless revealed thousands of falsified documents, thousands of unrecorded transactions, efforts to conceal losses of several billion dollars, and the fact that BCCI had apparently never made a profit. These revelations sent British bank examiners reeling. Unlike America, which insures deposits of up to one hundred thousand dollars per person, per institution, Britain only insured a maximum of twenty-five thousand dollars per deposit. Obviously, the Bank of England was within its power to immediately freeze BCCI activities in Britain, and that's exactly what Leigh-Pemberton did.

The various investigations by the DEA, the IRS, the Bank of England, and the New York County District Attorney's Office turned up conclusive evidence of BCCI having "loaned" CCAH stockholders the entire amounts used to purchase their CCAH investments. Just as it had done when Ghaith Pharaon had borrowed the funds to buy Bert Lance's stock in National Bank of Georgia, and as it had done for the Mahfouz brothers and countless other Arabs, BCCI had proven once again that it was nothing more than an enormous Ponzi scheme.[46]

The CIA-BCCI Connection

The Central Intelligence Agency has had intelligence on key political, economic, and social activities in the Middle East since the 1950s. One reason for this has been the importance of Arab oil to the U.S. economy. Even before OPEC was formed and the 1973 embargo was spearheaded by King Faisal, partially in retaliation for President Nixon's recalcitrance in defying Saudi demands that the U.S. quit giving aid to Israel, the Arabs had played a key, if somewhat subdued role, in international politics.

However, with the 1973 embargo came claims of a genuine domestic oil shortage, fueling anti-Semitic sentiment. The CIA knew better. It knew the "shortage" was nothing more than a clever subterfuge. What had actually taken place was a series of geologically and technically mandated oil production cutbacks in this country. In a political atmosphere charged with anti-Semitic sentiment in one camp and anti-Arab sentiment in another, the CIA was theoretically responsible for the protection of American interests abroad.

It was from the CIA that the Reagan administration first learned of the Saudis' desire to buy AWACs and F-15 fighter jets. The sale was actually completed while

President Reagan was recuperating from the gunshot wounds he had incurred during an assassination attempt. Soon after the embargo was in effect, dozens of former U.S. Embassy employees, Treasury Department attaches, Commerce Department analysts, army officers, Customs agents, and even former CIA station chiefs, joined the gold rush, jumping at the chance to stay in the Middle East and enjoy the perks being doled out by the Arab nouveau riche.[47]

As early as the 1950s and 1960s, the CIA had secretly funded pro-Arab organizations in the U.S. One, called Amideast (which was originally known as American Friends of the Middle East) was formed in the early 1950s. The CIA funded Amideast in the 1950s and 1960s through the nonprofit, tax-exempt Dearborn Foundation. In 1982, the Washington office of Amideast had displays containing pamphlets promoting a film entitled "Occupied Palestine," which argued that the Arabs had a right to all of Israel. But, if the 1950s and 1960s were decades of subtle CIA support for the Arab cause in the Middle East, the 1970s and 1980s were decades of entrenched CIA involvement in the Arab business world. This involvement eventually increased to the point of being inconsistent with the agency's purpose. Funneling arms to an organized militia fighting a war against Communist aggression on its own soil was one thing. Using an Arab-owned bank—known best for its fraudulent attempts to get a foothold in the American banking industry, for its Ponzi schemes, and for its drug money-laundering activities—as a vehicle for funding the clandestine activities of ruthless mercenaries like Barry Seal and Emile Camp, was quite another.

It cannot be denied that the CIA bent over backward on many occasions to camouflage some of BCCI's more nefarious activities. One example of this was in October 1978 when the Federal Reserve Board was considering the fraudulent application—prepared by Clark Clifford and his partner, Robert Altman—for the hostile takeover of Financial General Bankshares, Inc., (later called First American Bankshares) ostensibly by three individuals: Kamal Adham, Faisal Saud al-Fulaij, and Abdullah Darwaish. Because the offer was being made by foreigners, the CIA, FBI, and SEC were all required to file reports, which would then be considered by the board as part of the decision-making process. Adham had been chief of Saudi Intelligence, yet that fact never appeared in the CIA's report. As a matter of fact, no negative information regarding the Financial General takeover was released by the CIA until September 1986 when other agencies, such as the IRS and the DEA, had begun to scratch the surface and discover certain serious improprieties in the way BCCI was doing business. Even at that, the CIA report didn't mention Adham's role in the intelligence community; it simply reflected that BCCI was engaged in money laundering and other unlawful acts and had secretly gained control over Financial General.

Another example of the CIA attempting to cover for BCCI occurred on 6 May 1982 in Washington. The U.S. House Subcommittee on Commerce, Consumer and Monetary Affairs had scheduled hearings that day to investigate questionable Arab investments in the U.S. One hour before the meeting began, twelve CIA security personnel entered the committee room. Ten more entered at 10:00 A.M. when the meeting was beginning. A certified shorthand reporter, employed by the House, recorded the hearings. As soon as the meeting was adjourned, a CIA agent took possession of the tapes, and eight agents escorted the reporter to his office to confiscate as many tapes and records as they could get their hands on. The CIA had apparently been instructed to take the tapes back to headquarters across the river in Langley to be stored and transcribed. It was later learned that two months earlier President Reagan had personally tried to intervene and stop the subcommittee from declassifying materials to be discussed during the hearing. While the CIA and Congress were wrangling about who had a lawful claim to them, the tapes mysteriously disappeared.[48]

In 1988, Robert Gates, then-deputy director of the CIA, advised C-Chase prosecutors that in September 1986 the CIA was well aware of BCCI's unlawful activities. According to an official report contained in CIA files, dated September 1986, BCCI was at the time known to be involved in "illicit banking activities, particularly those related to narco-finance in the Western Hemisphere." The report went on to say that the drug money-laundering activities seemed to be concentrated in the Cayman Islands. One of CIA Director William Webster's final acts as director was to order a full review of the CIA's dealings with BCCI. Around the same time, Richard Kerr, then-deputy director of the CIA, told a high-school group the CIA had used BCCI for years to pay for covert operations. This was the money Barry Seal referred to as "trafficker funds."[49]

BCCI worked hard to make the right political, social, and business connections wherever it had a branch, or sought to establish one. That was especially true in America, where Hasan Abedi had to walk a tightrope, not only because of Bank of America's withdrawal as a stockholder in 1977 in the wake of the first negative Price-Waterhouse report, but also because the Arab oil embargo of 1973, which, ironically, was the source of the "new" Arab money, had also worked to inculcate a certain degree of mistrust of Arabs in the West.

Abedi was a Muslim visionary. He had visions of grandeur in regard to his own fate. He had visions of building an international banking empire based on Moslem theology and religious principles. And, he had a vision that this vast banking empire, making public donations to charitable organizations and helping provide start-up capital for high-profile business ventures in the Third World, could make dreams come true in developing nations. He nearly succeeded. But, the sins of men like Hasan Abedi and Charles Ponzi have ways of finding them. In the face of overwhelming evidence against it, BCCI pleaded guilty in December 1991 to federal and state criminal charges and forfeited $550 million to help repay foreign depositors and shore up the two struggling American banks it had secretly controlled. No financial institution in American history had been required to repay so much by a court of law.

Today, BCCI is owned by its first shareholder, Sheik Zayed of Abu Dhabi. He delivered Agha Hasan Abedi's former second in command, Swaleh Naqvi, to federal prosecutors in May 1994. Whether Sheik Zayed will ever be able to raise the BCCI phoenix from the ashes remains to be seen. But, as long as there are political influence peddlers and power brokers, like the Jackson Stephens and the Clark Cliffords of this world, he at least has a shot at it.

Endnotes

1. James Ring Adams and Douglas Frantz, *A Full Service Bank (How BCCI Stole Millions Around the World)* (NY: Pocket Books, 1992), 5, 296.

2. Ibid., 4, 5.

3. Steven Emerson, *The American House of Saud* (New York, Toronto, London, Sydney: Franklin Watts, 1985), 27.

4. Ibid., 35.

5. Ibid., 13.

6. Biographers of Adolf Hitler almost without exception contend that he read the *Protocols*, and believed them to be valid.

7. If nothing else, the *Protocols* make for interesting reading. Protocol no. 1 states that political rights are based on force, and nothing else. There's no such thing as freedom; there is only power. Protocol no. 2 states that whoever controls the press, controls the power to influence the people. Protocols no. 3 and 5 encourage the questioning of democratic authority, and a "free marketplace of ideas," the ultimate goal of which is to confuse opinion and bankrupt the state. Protocol no. 4 supports the idea of religion, so long as it recognizes the inequality of all men, and is based on faith in math and science, rather than in God. Protocol no. 5 also supports the idea of a strong central government, placed ultimately in the hands of an oligarchy. Protocol no. 6 promotes the establishment of monopolies and a super government. The masses are to become dependent on the largess of that government. Protocol no. 13 urges the encouragement of liberal thinking until the time is ripe for a complete overthrow of all democratic institutions. Protocol no. 16 undermines the idea of constitutionalism, and urges higher education consistent with the protocols.

8. Emerson, *House of Saud*, 52, 53.

9. Ibid., 56.

10. Ibid., 72, 73.

11. Ibid., 80, 82, 100.

12. Ibid., 187, 197, 201.

13. Ibid., 217, 268, 300, 301, 737; Adams and Frantz, *A Full Service Bank*, 165.

14. Emerson, *House of Saud*, 116, 117.

15. There is some question as to whether or not Financial General actually controlled National Bank of Georgia. Adams and Frantz don't mention this in their book, *A Full Service Bank*. L.J. Davis, however, contends that it did, in a piece entitled "The Name of Rose," *The New Republic*, 4 April 1994. Davis is probably correct. Adams and Frantz's error is likely just an oversight.

16. Emerson, *House of Saud*, 166, 117.

17. Ibid., 6, 91.

18. Adams and Frantz, *Full Service Bank*, 7, 10.

19. Ibid., 13-15.

20. Ibid., 19.

21. Ibid., 20-22.

22. Ibid., 22-29.

23. Ibid., 31, 32; Emerson, *House of Saud*, 118.

24. Adams and Frantz, *Full Service Bank*, 32.

25. Ibid., 54, 55.

26. By the beginning of 1977, Bank of America was so happy with its BCCI investment that it bought enough stock to give it an interest of 40 percent in BCCI. But that same year, a Price-Waterhouse accounting audit at BCCI's headquarters branch in London, revealed highly questionable loan policies, including an extension of $80 million in totally unsecured credit to the Gokal shipping family. Such loans, common among Arabs, were totally unacceptable in the West. See, Adams and Frantz, *Full Service Bank*, 38-43.

27. Ibid., 33-39; Emerson, *House of Saud*, 72.

28. Adams and Frantz, *Full Service Bank*, 49-52.

29. Ibid., 56.

30. Emerson, *House of Saud*, 117.

31. Adams and Frantz, *Full Service Bank*, 64, 65.

32. Ibid., 68. Title 12, U.S. Code, Section 1823, et seq., and the *D'Oench, Duhme* doctrine, provide that secret side agreements are not a bar to actions enforcing obligations when those actions are brought by the federal government in its capacity as receiver.

33. Ibid., 74, 268.

34. Ibid., 32.

35. Ibid., 38-43, 53.

36. Ibid., 53, 70.

37. Ibid., 83. Adams and Frantz also describe a similar money-making scam which was the brainchild of mob boss, Meyer Lansky, who referred to it as a "loan back," and spent forty years trying to perfect it. Ibid., 84.

38. Ibid., 105.

39. Ibid., 88, 89.

40. Ibid., 90.

41. Ibid., 94, 97, 98.

42. Ibid., 105, 106.

43. Ibid., 116, 133.

44. Ibid., 142, 76, 77, 82.

45. Ibid., 282, 188.

46. Ibid., 315, 291.

47. Emerson, *House of Saud*, 127-128, 260.

48. Ibid., 313, 314.

49. Adams and Frantz, *Full Service Bank*, 238, 323.

Chapter Six

Happy Days—
Ponzi Comes to the
Land of Opportunity

The problems the DEA, IRS, and other government agencies were having in dealing with BCCI were similar to the problems the agencies faced in Arkansas when they were attempting to gather evidence to convict Barry Seal. The left hand of government didn't seem to know what the right hand was doing and didn't seem to care. The IRS CID had been ready to pounce on BCCI in Miami in 1985 because it had solid evidence of the failure of a bank connected to BCCI to file CTRs, in violation of the federal Bank Secrecy Act of 1970.[1] But, shortly after an undercover investigation by CID agents was approved, the plans were called off by someone in Washington. The same type of thing was occurring in Arkansas in the 1980s and was directly related to the problems the DEA and IRS were having with BCCI and BCCI-related activities everywhere.

The main reason Barry Seal started his smuggling activities in Mena, Arkansas, in 1981, was that the Mena Intermountain Regional Airport was equipped to do retrofitting, and if a pilot landed an aircraft there specifically for retrofitting, U.S. Customs wouldn't inspect the plane, its crew, its passengers, or its cargo. Such safe harbors were extremely rare, and thus very attractive to drug smugglers and gun runners. The lack of any conspicuous presence on the part of U.S. Customs also drew Seal to the private airport in Opa-Locka, Florida, from time to time, but Arkansas was a lot closer to home.

Seal had another reason to do business in Arkansas: a large market for the drugs he brought back each time he flew to Central and South America. In the beginning, Seal flew guns and explosives to Mexico, returning with sacks of cash in payment for his efforts. But, it was only natural that a soldier of fortune like Seal would discover that he could make even more money by transporting other types of contraband. As time went on, he would find a solid market for smuggling automatic weapons into Nicaragua and smuggling white powder out.

At that time, the Nicaraguan government was controlled by a group of ruthless Communists calling itself the Government of National Reconstruction of Nicaragua, better known as the Sandinistas. They would do practically anything for money to finance their continuing revolution, and Seal knew it. The CIA knew it too. It didn't take Seal long to begin making connections in Nicaragua, Panama, and Colombia to facilitate a new smuggling activity. Nothing was more lucrative than cocaine, and nowhere was it easier to find than Colombia. All that was needed was a connection between Colombia and Nicaragua. The Medellin cartel would see to it that that happened. And, the CIA agreed to quietly look away.[2]

Aiding the Contras

In the early days, Seal made hundreds of smuggling trips back and forth to Panama, Nicaragua, El Salvador, Costa Rica, and Honduras, practically without incident. His usual runs involved weapons and ordnance. But, he could easily be persuaded to smuggle drugs as well. Drug smuggling was risky business. In 1979, Seal found out just how risky when the Honduran government arrested him on drug-trafficking charges. He met fellow-Louisianian and fellow-pilot Emile Camp for the first time when the two were placed in the same jail cell. On their return, Seal and Camp went into business together although Seal adamantly denied under oath that they were ever partners. Camp was an accomplished pilot in his own right and soon proved that he could also be trusted with a complete understanding of Seal's smuggling operations and the network of people involved in it.[3]

Sometime in 1982 or early 1983, Seal was approached by the CIA about smuggling guns to Nicaragua. The ninety-eighth Congress had passed H.R. 2760, commonly known as the Boland Amendment, and it put a halt to the CIA's more overt activities in Nicaragua. The purpose of the Boland Amendment was as follows:

> To amend the Intelligence Authorization Act for Fiscal Year 1983 to prohibit United States support for military or paramilitary operations in Nicaragua and to authorize assistance, to be openly provided to governments of countries in Central America, to interdict the supply of military equipment from Nicaragua and Cuba to individuals, groups, organizations, or movements seeking to overthrow governments of countries in Central America.

With the passage of Boland, the death knell sounded on the flow of arms and ordnance to the Nicaraguan Freedom Fighters. The intelligence community was essentially being told by Congress to limit its activities to assisting the governments of Central America in inhibiting the flow of weapons to the Sandinistas from places like Cuba, which were sympathetic to the revolution. Taking the additional step of actually supplying arms to the Contras was now prohibited.

Of particular importance to CIA operations in Nicaragua were the following prohibitions. Title VIII, Section 801(a) of Public Law (P.L.) 98-215, provided that no funds appropriated for fiscal years 1983 or 1984 for the CIA or "any other department, agency, or entity of the United States involved in intelligence activities" could be spent in supporting "military or paramilitary operations in or against Nicaragua." The sanctions to be imposed for the violation of the act included a potentially massive withdrawal of funding for CIA operations in general.

During the time the U.S. government was involved in the Nicaraguan conflict, in the early and mid-1980s, Congress and the president seesawed back and forth in their policy considerations. While the Boland Amendment completely prohibited U.S. support of military or paramilitary operations in Nicaragua, in 1984, P.L. 98-215 changed the government's position by putting a ceiling of $24 million on appropriations for covert assistance for military operations in Nicaragua:

> During fiscal year 1984, not more than $24,000,000 of the funds available to the Central Intelligence Agency, the Department of Defense, or any other agency or entity of the United States involved in intelligence activities may be . . . expended for the purpose . . . of supporting . . . military or paramilitary operations in Nicaragua by any nation, group, organization, movement, or individual.[4]

Mercenaries like Barry Seal and Emile Camp were only too happy to receive some of that money.

Apparently, between 1983 and 1984, Congress realized a few things about the character, credibility, and trustworthiness of the Sandinistas. Congress found in 1984 that the so-called Government of National Reconstruction of Nicaragua had "failed to keep solemn promises, made to the Organization of American States in July 1979, to establish full respect for human rights and political liberties." Congress then called for the president to convene a meeting of the OAS ministers to discuss the problem.

What all of that meant for the CIA in 1983 was that if the U.S. government was going to help the Nicaraguan Freedom Fighters in any way, it would have to be done very quietly. And, at the time, despite the presence of its Intermountain Regional Airport, Mena, Arkansas, was one of the quietest places in the country.

There are varying accounts of how Barry Seal and the CIA initially met to discuss what apparently became known as Operation Centaur Rose. Most involve speculation that's unfounded, if not completely unbelievable. Seal was well known in drug-trafficking and gun-running circles as a barn stormer and daredevil. His younger brother Benjy once said if Barry was out of fuel and needed to land immediately and learned of a second airstrip—no matter how secluded—ten miles away, he would opt for the second strip just to see if he could make it. Known for his brazen audacity, Seal also made no bones about where his "hideout" in the swamp was. He even put up a four-by-eight-foot FAA warning sign on his landing strip in Louisiana, bearing the inscription "A.B. Seal, Owner" in large bold letters. Seal was also a legend among pilots, having been the youngest in U.S. history to be given a commercial command; then being the youngest to command a Boeing 747 crew. That kind of reputation follows a man around. And, the CIA was well aware of it.[5]

If the Boland Amendment represented the "letter" of the law, blocking the CIA's road to Nicaragua, the agency would have to rely on the "spirit" of other laws to circumvent that obstruction. It's safe to say that the main purpose of the CIA is to gather intelligence regarding the overt and covert operations of foreign governments and organized nongovernmental groups and apply that intelligence in whatever way is necessary to best protect U.S. interests worldwide. In the minds of intelligence personnel, trained in avoiding legal pitfalls crafted in starchy government offices, the ends often justified the means. If U.S. intelligence used forged documents, bogus passports, and carried unlawful weapons in places like the eastern European Communist bloc, in defiance of their laws and in defiance of well-accepted international protocol, why wouldn't the same principles apply to Nicaragua? Weren't the Sandinistas a threat to democracy in the region? They were indeed. And, to the CIA, that made them fair game.

In 1982, being keenly aware of who Barry Seal was and what he was doing, the CIA approached him with an offer. If he would begin running guns and ordnance to Nicaragua to arm the freedom fighters, he would be paid handsomely, and he would still be able to haul the cargo of his choosing on the return flights. (If Terry Reed's account is true, it's quite possible that one of the CIA operatives with whom Seal initially came in contact was retired U.S. Marine Lt. Col. Oliver North, who, according to Reed, was using the code name "John Cathey" at the time.)[6] Barry Seal's sense of patriotism and propriety may have been rife for scrutiny in 1982 (there's absolutely nothing patriotic or proper about drug smuggling), but his sense of smell for greenbacks was as keen as ever. The deal presented by the CIA must have been a good one because Barry Seal accepted the offer. Of course, it's highly likely that the CIA dropped a few subtle hints about the possibility of the DEA investigating Seal should he fail to cooperate, but Seal was not one to fear arrest. Having been arrested several times and convicted at least twice—once in Louisiana and once in Florida—the prospect of being arrested again didn't seem to phase him.[7]

A Chicken in Every Pot

As a drug trafficker, Barry Seal had significant contacts with the people he supplied. In Arkansas, a handful of names that appeared in social registers and in silk-stocking, country-club circles also appeared in Barry Seal's little black book as customers. Among them were Dan Lasater, Don Tyson, Roger Clinton, and, if Terry Reed and Larry Nichols are to be believed, Arkansas Gov. Bill Clinton.

By all accounts, between 1980 and 1986, Seal had smuggled at least 36 metric tons of cocaine, 104 tons of marijuana, and 3 tons of heroin into Arkansas. That kind of volume, and the black money associated with it, required a vast money-laundering network and the cooperation of certain people in key positions in state government, and Arkansas had both.

In 1985, the Arkansas Development Finance Authority (ADFA) was created by State Legislative Act 1062. The brainchild of Bill Clinton, with input from several lawyers at the Rose Law Firm, including Hillary Rodham Clinton, Webb Hubbell, and Vince Foster, three of the firm's specialists in commercial law and securities, ADFA's first office was in the same building with James B. McDougal's thrift, Madison Guaranty Savings & Loan Association. Hubbell actually prepared and drafted the enabling legislation that created ADFA. The ten-member ADFA board was appointed by the governor. The Rose Law Firm and Stephens, Inc., were well represented on the board.[8]

ADFA's official purpose was to secure financing at below-market rates for agricultural business enterprises,

capital improvements, health-care facilities, housing developments, and industrial enterprises, guaranteeing the
loans with the credit of the state of Arkansas. The last
purpose mentioned—financing industrial enterprises—was
an important one for the CIA because it enabled small
industries in Arkansas to begin manufacturing parts used
in converting semiautomatic rifles into fully automatic
rifles. One of the first ADFA-arranged loans was to Park-
O-Meter, Inc. (POM), on 31 December 1985 in the
amount of $2.75 million. Seth Ward, who owned POM,
was Webb Hubbell's father-in-law.[9]

The Ward family had been in the manufacturing
industry for years in Arkansas. Business was booming in
the mid-1970s when multi-million dollar orders from
Saudi Arabia and Egypt boosted the production at Ward
Industries of Conway by 25 percent.

Hubbell was on the board of directors of POM when
the ADFA loan was issued. The Rose Law Firm prepared
the closing documents to complete the transaction for a
substantial fee. Interestingly, Webb Hubbell was also on
the board of ADFA when the POM loan was made.[10] He
thus served in three different, mutually exclusive capaci-
ties: as representative of ADFA, the agency facilitating
the loan; as agent for POM, the company receiving the
funds; and as closing attorney. A more flagrant, patent,
conflict of interest can scarcely be imagined, yet this was
a man who'd served as chief justice of the Arkansas
Supreme Court and was one of the governor's closest
friends.

Arkansas is a small state with a large grapevine.
Hubbell was well aware, as was Bill Clinton and the
others in their circle of friends, that the CIA's operation
had been going on for some time and that Iver Johnson's
and Brodix Manufacturing had been casting M-16 conversion kits for months. In fact, at least one former IRS
CID special agent and one former Arkansas State Police
special investigator maintain that in order to obtain the

cooperation of state government, the CIA was required to pay 10 percent of the profits from the cocaine and arms trade to the state. When Seth Ward began to get wind of the enormous profits to be made in the illegal arms trade, he demanded that POM have a slice of the CIA pie. Until 1986, POM had manufactured parking meters at its plant in Russellville, Arkansas. With the ADFA money, the company was able to expand its operations. Its corporate minutes reflected that the expansion was necessary to "accommodate new government contracts." Soon, POM was subcontracting with Iver Johnson's to build five hundred M-16 bolt and carrier assemblies per month for transport to Nicaragua. ADFA had made Seth Ward's dream a reality.[11]

ADFA's apparent altruism was belied by the fact that most of the loans brokered through ADFA ended up benefiting private companies and individuals who were close to Bill and Hillary Clinton. The POM loan is a prime example of this. Moreover, the Rose Law Firm seems to have been the only firm entrusted with closing ADFA-related loans. With each closing, Rose made as much as fifty thousand dollars, regardless of the size of the loan. From 1985 to 1992, at least $7 billion, and as much as $18 billion (depending on the source) in state bonds were issued through ADFA, including loans to companies like Seth Ward's Park-O-Meter, Inc.[12] Each recipient had some tie to Clinton or supported his campaigns. His 1990 gubernatorial campaign received over four hundred thousand dollars from companies that had stood in the ADFA bread line.[13]

Larry Nichols, the former director of marketing for ADFA, has alleged that after spending two months preparing ADFA's annual report, he noticed that the borrowers weren't paying interest on their loans. He then reviewed the records in more detail and made the amazing discovery that the accounts were being zeroed out—as though payments were being made—when in fact no payments of any kind were being made. Yet, at the same time, millions of dollars continued to pour into ADFA's accounts, and millions more were distributed through additional bond issues. Rose continued to close each transaction. Little Rock-based bond brokers, like Stephens, Inc., did the underwriting.[14] These allegations have a definite ring of truth to them, not only because Nichols was an ADFA insider, but also because like BCCI, ADFA was nothing more than a high-powered Ponzi scheme. The question is, why would ADFA be run like BCCI? Were there any connections between the two financial organizations?

Arkansas Royalty

In a state known more for hillbilly theme parks like Dogpatch, USA, and fast-pace college basketball played before cacophonous crowds of "Hee-Haw" types attempting to imitate the call of the razorback hog, the Stephens family is a diamond in the rough. It can safely be said that they own most of Arkansas, and what they don't own, they control. From Worthen Bank and Arkla Petroleum to Stephens, Inc., their influence reaches every hill and "holler" from El Dorado to Yellville. Although their rise to power was not the Horatio Alger story every American enjoys hearing, they definitely made the most of what they had to start with.

The sons of A.J. Stephens, a sometime state legislator who was a lifelong force in the Democratic party (the only party in one-party Arkansas), Wilton "Mr. Witt" and Jackson were born sixteen years apart. They were raised on a cotton farm in Plattsville, Arkansas. Mr. Witt, the oldest, grew up watching his father dabble in politics and oil stocks. He quit school in the eighth grade, deciding it was a waste of time. Selling Bibles door-to-door, he discovered, more by accident than anything else, that a lot of money could be made in a short amount of time in the securities trade. He began with municipal bonds.

As the story goes, he found some old bond certificates in a box in his father's house and took them to a broker out of curiosity. The broker acted like they were worthless and offered to take them off Mr. Witt's hands. Suspicious, Mr. Witt decided to keep them. He later sold them for a handsome amount and used some of the money to buy stock in a natural gas company. The company would later become Arkla, and Mr. Witt would later own the company.

In 1933, Mr. Witt borrowed $15,000 (a small fortune at the time) to establish a brokerage firm that would sell, among other securities, municipal bonds. The investment proved to be the right move because the bond market grew under Roosevelt's New Deal until the value of discounted bonds tripled.

Jackson Stephens was a very good student. The antithesis of his older brother, who did business with a handshake, a wink, and a promise, Jack was careful and methodical. His efforts were rewarded with an appointment to the United States Naval Academy when he graduated from high school. At the academy, he roomed with another country boy, midshipman James Earl Carter of Plains, Georgia. Plattsville and Plains had a lot in common; so did Carter and Stephens. After their graduation in 1946, they remained friends over the years, with Stephens being one of Carter's chief political supporters both in his campaigns for governor of Georgia and for president of the United States.

As a child, watching his father make deals by chewing the fat with Democratic party bigwigs, and as an adult, watching his brother become a king maker in his own right, Jackson Stephens learned the value of being politically connected. He was instrumental in six-term Arkansas Gov. Orval Faubus' political career. He frequently supported U.S. Sen. J. William Fulbright during his thirty-year career in Congress. Fulbright in turn helped Stephens establish ties to the Middle East, which enhanced his relationship with Jimmy Carter, Bert Lance, and Hasan Abedi of BCCI. It was while they were both working on Fulbright's staff in Washington that James McDougal, the future owner of Madison Guaranty Savings & Loan Association, and Bill Clinton first met and became friends. Sen. Dale Bumpers was also a Stephens-supported Arkansas Democrat.

The spoils of political victory were good to Jackson Stephens. After he was elected president, Carter rewarded Stephens by helping him make key connections in the banking industry. It was through Carter that Stephens was introduced to Bert Lance. It was through Carter that Stephens invested in Financial General Bankshares, Inc., the holding company which controlled National Bank of Georgia. And, it was through Carter that Stephens met Abedi, who was president and CEO of BCCI. Stephens would ultimately help broker the sale of Bert Lance's 120,000 shares of stock in National Bank of Georgia (NGB) to yet another Carter acquaintance, Ghaith Pharaon.

The NBG stock sale was only the tip of the proverbial iceberg. Stephens didn't just broker the sale of Lance's stock to Pharaon, he put together the entire deal, including the sale of blocks of 4.9 percent each of the stock in Financial General. With the help of Joseph Giroir, at the time the Rose Law Firm's securities law expert, Stephens knew that 4.9 percent was the maximum allowed per block if the expense of registration with the SEC, and under the Arkansas "Blue Sky" laws, was to be avoided. Although Jackson Stephens made only a small personal profit from the sale of his 5 percent interest in Financial General, and Stephens, Inc. made a broker's fee of about ninety-five thousand dollars, Stephens had done a great favor to Lance, Carter, and Abedi. Later on, the SEC would investigate the ties between the Stephens and BCCI. The case never went to trial. Instead, the Stephens settled through a plea bargain agreement.

During the same time period, Jack Stephens was introduced by Robert B. Anderson, President Eisenhower's secretary of the Treasury, to Indonesian business magnate, Mochtar Riady. Riady was always looking for investments and contributed to Bill Clinton's presidential campaign in 1992 through one of his companies. Anderson had an ulterior motive however. He had just opened an offshore bank on Anguilla called Commercial and Trade Bank and Trust, Ltd. The bank catered to the super rich and drug-money launderers, a fact that would ultimately land Anderson in prison. Stephens eventually did business with Anderson, but he was hesitant to get involved with Riady. Like Hasan Abedi, Mochtar Riady wanted to make inroads into the American banking industry. When Riady learned that stock in Financial General was for sale, he too expressed an interest, but it was not to be. When President Clinton went to Indonesia in November 1994, he paid a special visit to Riady's people. That may have been his primary reason for making the trip.

While with the Rose Law Firm, Joseph Giroir lobbied the Arkansas legislature to change the laws to loosen restrictions on the banking industry. The suggested changes were adopted, and Stephens immediately began filing charters for large bank holding companies. One new holding company, Worthen Banking Corporation, was formed by Stephens and a new partner, Mochtar Riady. When Riady flashed $25 million at him, Stephens reconsidered doing business with the Indonesians. Worthen was actually formed when First Arkansas Bankcorp, in which Stephens and Riady had placed a sizeable investment, merged with another group of banks owned by Giroir. This particular endeavor proved costly. In 1985, Worthen became a major depository of Arkansas state tax receipts, and quietly lost $52 million, all of which represented tax receipts, by investing it with an unscrupulous churning operation in New Jersey. The money was never recovered, and Worthen almost went under, but a bailout from stockholders saved the day. Amazingly, neither the New Jersey people, nor Stephens, nor Riady, was ever prosecuted, largely due to a strange quirk of Arkansas law. The governor, not the state attorney general or the county prosecutors, has the sole power to convene a grand jury. Yet, in Ohio in 1985, several people associated with a savings bank, under similar circumstances, were convicted on securities fraud charges for absconding with a lot less than $52 million.[15]

There are those who are also convinced that Jackson Stephens was as much a part of the cocaine trade as anyone else in Little Rock in the 1980s, and they're probably right. In fact, the DEA apparently has a file on Stephens which refers to him as a cocaine and alcohol abuser.[16] Those would be strong words, except for the fact that when IRS CID Special Agent William Duncan and Arkansas State Police Special Investigator Russell Welch presented evidence to the U.S. attorney and encouraged him to convene a grand jury to look into the obvious drug-trafficking activities taking place in and around Mena, he was suddenly pulled off the case. At the time, according to former CIA operative Robert Johnson, Stephens put indirect pressure on U.S. Attorney General Edwin Meese to appoint J. Michael Fitzhugh as U.S. attorney for the western district of Arkansas. Fitzhugh followed orders and effectively stonewalled the investigations, but not necessarily because he was part of any kind of conspiracy to cover up the Mena smuggling activities or to inhibit legitimate police work. Barry Seal may very well have had some input into the changing of the guard at the federal courthouse. He claimed to have bribed Meese on numerous occasions to keep federal investigators from successfully prosecuting him. Seal also claimed that he paid everyone he could have possibly influenced from the U.S. Attorney to the sheriffs of rural Arkansas counties.[17]

Another force to be reckoned with in Arkansas politics to this day is Donald J. Tyson, president and CEO of Tyson Foods, Inc., America's largest fowl producer. Tyson may also be one of America's largest cocaine traffickers, and his intimacy with the White House should have given rise to public outrage long before the debacle involving former Agriculture Secretary Michael Espy.[18]

In December 1994, Tyson's former number-two pilot told Donald Smaltz, the independent counsel investigating the Espy case, that on six occasions he carried envelopes with stacks of hundred-dollar bills to Little Rock, where the money was transferred to Clinton, who was governor at the time. Believed to be payoffs of some sort, Whitewater independent counsel Kenneth Starr was looking into the matter in early 1995.

Both state law enforcement authorities in Arkansas and the U.S. DEA have extensive files on Don Tyson. One DEA report, dated 10 March 1984 and prepared by Tucson, Arizona, police, contains the following language:

> On July 5, 1984 [code name for narcotics officer] telephoned [Special Agent] Anthony Coulson at the Tucson District Office [of the DEA] concerning narcotic trafficking by Donald J. TYSON in and around the area of Fayetteville, Arkansas. The Cooperating Individual (CI) [an informant] had information concerning *heroin, cocaine and marijuana trafficking in the States of Arkansas, Texas, and Missouri by the TYSON Organization.* [emphasis added][19]

The report goes on to charge that two men, named Montez and Kehr, are "believed to be Lieutenants for Donald TYSON" and that Montez sells cocaine through his restaurant in Tucson.

Also mentioned in the report is a place called the Barn, located between Springdale (headquarters of Tyson Foods) and Fayetteville, which Tyson allegedly used as a "stash" location for "large quantities of marijuana and cocaine." Tyson was also known to have meetings at the Ramada Inn in Fayetteville, "concerning the business in and around THE BARN."[20] Among those known to have frequented the Barn are Dan Lasater, Roger Clinton, Barry Seal, and Bill Clinton.

Another DEA report, dated 1 January 1983, was prepared by Special Agent Dean Gates with the Oklahoma City DEA Office. The report states that a known cocaine dealer operating in Tulsa, named Jerry Prideaux, was being supplied by Don Tyson. It was the manner in which the cocaine was being transported that surprised the DEA:

> Sgt. Myres advised that he had received information from confidential sources indicating that PRIDEAUX' source for cocaine is Don TYSON, who owns TYSON INDUSTRIES in Springdale, Arkansas. Sgt. Myres also advised that his source said that TYSON *smuggles cocaine from Colombia, South America inside race horses to Hot Springs, Arkansas.* [emphasis added][21]

If the DEA didn't purport to have a clue as to how Tyson transported racehorses with bellies full of white powder from Colombia to Arkansas, it didn't need to look much farther than Mena Intermountain Regional Airport. That's where Barry Seal landed The Fat Lady, and The Fat Lady could transport a herd of horses without even batting an eyelash. A woman who lived next door to Seal's "camp" (at one time a very plush two-story lodge on the banks of the Amite River in a swamp) believes Seal did transport horses. From her second-floor sun deck, she often watched The Fat Lady land on Seal's huge grass airstrip. A couple of times she was astonished to see horses led out of the airplane, walked around, allowed to graze, and finally led back into the hulking fuselage for the flight to parts unknown.[22]

It's no secret in Arkansas that Tyson pumped tens of thousands of dollars into Bill Clinton's initial gubernatorial campaign in Arkansas in the late 1980s. What isn't as well known is that Tyson, likewise, made sure Clinton was not reelected in 1982. Not surprisingly, strings were always attached to Tyson's support, and as governor, Clinton had failed to deliver on a promise to relax trucking and environmental regulations which would've significantly reduced the general and administrative expenses on Tyson's balance sheet. But, being a quick learner, Clinton did deliver the next time he was elected. The second time around, it only cost Tyson a fifteen-thousand-dollar campaign contribution and a promise that his legal counsel, James Blair, would help Hillary Rodham Clinton earn some very quick dividends on the commodities exchange. Tyson was true to his word. Carefully following Blair's advice, Rodham Clinton turned a one-thousand-dollar investment into one hundred thousand dollars, practically in record time.[23]

In spite of Tyson's clearly documented political influence peddling and known drug-trafficking activities, the Springdale poultry magnate to whom the DEA affectionately refers as the Chicken Man has never been prosecuted. One reason may be that when it comes to prosecution by the state in Arkansas, only the governor has the authority to convene a grand jury. And, in the past, when well-intentioned U.S. attorneys have attempted to embark on serious investigations into these types of racketeering activities, there has either been an immediate changing of the guard or the erection of an insurmountable stone wall. Whether such things are the results of bribery, Bubba-ism, or good old-fashioned political chicanery, one thing is abundantly clear: in Arkansas, king makers, like Jackson Stephens and Don Tyson, are treated like kings.

A Ponzi Scheme in Arkansas

In the mid-1980s, cocaine trafficking was perhaps the most lucrative business in the land of opportunity.

The cocky Barry Seal coolly admitted in federal court that he was making $25 million a year smuggling guns and dope in and out of Mena. That he was making considerably more is evident from a report in the summer of 1994 that one of his bank accounts at Fuji Bank in the Cayman Islands reflected a balance $1.645 billion. Seal only admitted making $25 million a year. In truth, he was making considerably more. He may have been paying that much annually in bribes to public officials.

At any rate, Don Tyson, Jackson Stephens, Dan Lasater, and especially Bill Clinton clearly understood the potential for gargantuan revenues if the state was to carefully design a complicated drug-trafficking and money-laundering operation, based on an underlying Ponzi scheme, and established under the watchful eye of Arkansas officials, and with virtually no resistance from the CIA. It would, of course, take a team effort to put it all together. It would require the help of the most skilled lawyers available, the cooperation of banks willing to ignore the Bank Secrecy Act of 1970 (calling for CTRs on certain cash transactions), bond brokers who understood banking as well as money laundering, politicians who could control law enforcement agencies and prosecutors, and an international bank, with offices outside the United States. With all of those ingredients in place, this handful of treacherous, power-hungry people would be in a position to easily control the state house and the banking industry. As if that weren't enough, they also made sure that, if necessary, witnesses could be disposed of, by controlling political appointments, like the state medical examiner, and by controlling elections for judges, prosecutors, and county sheriffs.

ADFA's purpose, as proclaimed in speeches by Bill Clinton, was to lure industry to Arkansas, by offering low-interest bond money. Theoretically, this would be a boon to employment and would increase tax revenues. ADFA was to be the knight in shining armor for those struggling business people who couldn't obtain loans for start-up capital anywhere else. But, ADFA's records re-flect a slightly different picture. By all accounts, only about sixty bond issues came through ADFA between 1985 and 1992. Most of those were to Clinton support-ers. Others went to charities and religious organizations. ADFA itself had dispensed $719 million through 1992, yielding fat commissions for local bond brokers and underwriters like Stephens, Inc.

It is highly likely that the inspiration for ADFA ini-tially came from Jackson Stephens. Being CEO of the largest investment brokerage firm west of Wall Street, having known Bert Lance and Hasan Abedi for about eight years, before ADFA was formed, having assisted BCCI in making its initial inroads in the American bank-ing industry by brokering the sale of National Bank of Georgia stock to BCCI straw-man Ghaith Pharaon, and having helped arrange the sale of Financial General Bankshares to BCCI stockholders Kamal Adham, Faisal Saud al-Fulaij, and Abdullah Darwaish, Stephens clearly understood how BCCI worked.

BCCI got its start in 1972 because Hasan Abedi had been able to persuade Middle Eastern oil magnates to invest in his bank by showing them that Bank of America, the world's largest private bank at the time, owned 25 percent of BCCI and by suggesting that they needed to "get in while the getting was good." Likewise, ADFA began with a $6 million capital infusion from the Arkan-sas State Treasury.[24] As was the case with BCCI, and all typical Ponzi schemes, ADFA never intended to repay the State Treasury.

According to Terry Reed and John Cummings, former CIA operative Robert Johnson has revealed that shortly after ADFA got its initial funding, the CIA agreed to use ADFA to launder the black money it received through arms sales to the freedom fighters. He says the "deal" cut with the Clinton administration in 1985 was that the CIA would pay 10 percent of the funds it received from Operation Centaur Rose (which was mainly Barry Seal's arms-smuggling operation) to ADFA, in exchange for the state's cooperation at all levels. For that percentage of the take, Bill Clinton would ensure that state and local law enforcement authorities wouldn't expose the CIA's operations, prompting Barry Seal to joke that Arkansas was "the only country north of Mexico where drug smugglers could get a police escort."[25] But, the CIA knew there were a dozen "Barney Fifes" in a dozen Arkansas hillbilly hamlets, and the last thing it needed was to have someone stumble over its operations. Clinton would make sure that wouldn't happen.

The CIA was to bring its 10 percent to bond broker Dan Lasater, who would then get it to ADFA. The money was routinely stuffed into heavy canvas duffle bags in Nicaragua and flown back either to the Mena airport, where it was loaded on smaller aircraft for transport to various locations in Arkansas and elsewhere, or it was actually dropped from planes like Barry Seal's Fat Lady over predetermined points. Seal also dropped sacks of cocaine, marijuana, and heroin, complete with electronic transmitters, on occasion, as a form of curb service to valued customers like Lasater. Seal's main drop target for Lasater was Seth Ward's Triple-S Ranch, just outside Little Rock. Ward's son-in-law, Finis Shellnut, actually lived at the ranch and physically retrieved the money. Lasater and Bill Clinton's brother, Roger, would also retrieve some of the flotsam and jetsam and eventually cart some or all of it to ADFA. The drugs would be sold or used by Lasater, Roger Clinton, and their circle of friends, which included Roger's brother, Bill.[26]

For several months in 1986, a woman named Jane Parks was the manager of the Vantage Point Apartments in Little Rock. Her office had at one time been a three-bedroom, two-bath apartment; a bedroom and bath having been walled off and converted into an office. During the summer of 1986, the apartment next door to that office was occupied by Bill Clinton's brother, Roger.

Ms. Parks was forced to call the police on many occasions that summer when tenants complained about the raucous all-night parties Clinton threw.

Parks has said that several times she entered Roger Clinton's apartment in connection with her various managerial duties and saw cocaine and a razor blade on a mirror, lying in open view on the coffee table in the center of the living room. She also reports that the apartment was frequented by young women and that, periodically, while these young women were in the apartment, Arkansas State Police units would arrive with Governor Clinton emerging and entering the apartment. Often Clinton wouldn't leave the apartment for hours. The police units would stay until the governor was ready to leave. Ms. Parks also believes she heard Bill Clinton's voice—through the thin layer of sheetrock separating the apartment from her office—remarking to Roger about the quality of some cocaine Roger had obviously provided. More out of fear than anything else, Ms. Parks began documenting these incidents. Her husband, Luther Gerald "Jerry" Parks, was a private investigator who ultimately obtained the contract to provide security for Bill Clinton's presidential campaign headquarters in Little Rock. Parks encouraged his wife to keep listening and taking notes. He wanted evidence of the activities in Roger Clinton's apartment in the event he ever had to clear himself or his family of any charges that might be leveled against them. A former police officer, Parks knew how things worked in Arkansas. In September 1993, Jerry Parks was shot to death in Little Rock as he drove home with a takeout order from an El Chico Mexican restaurant.[27]

In addition to Little Rock and Mena, drug deliveries were made in Polk and Saline Counties, where the level of drug-related political corruption was as high as anywhere in the state. One August night, a year and a half after Seal was gunned down, two teen-aged boys, Kevin Ives and Don Henry, were suspiciously run over by a

Union Pacific freight train near the town of Alexander, in Saline County, near the Pulaski County line.

Arkansas Medical Examiner Fahmy Malak, a Clinton appointee and close friend of the governor, ruled the deaths a double suicide and reported that each boy had large quantities of tetrahydrocannabinol, the hallucinogen contained in marijuana, in their blood. The findings were totally unacceptable to the boys' families, and a second medical examination was performed by an independent forensic pathologist. The second report revealed knife wounds in the body of one of the boys and a severe blow to the head of the other. The wounds were determined to have taken place hours before the train rolled over their bodies. Drug trafficking activity was known to occur in the wee hours of the morning in that part of the state.[28]

ADFA's growth as a Ponzi scheme was commensurate with the increase in deposits from the CIA's tithe, and from the black money from drug sales that ADFA helped launder. As of January 1995, no one, with the possible exception of Whitewater independent counsel Kenneth W. Starr, knew just how much money the CIA might have pumped into ADFA, but it's a safe bet that it exceeded $250 million—the amount received in a two-year period in the late 1980s.[29]

As brokerage firms like Stephens, Inc., began to roll along smoothly and fit comfortably into the ADFA scheme, enormous amounts of money were loaned through bond issues to Clinton supporters, who lined up to milk the ADFA cow. These funds also lined the pockets of the Rose Law Firm's retirement plan. The loan beneficiaries then made their contributions to whatever Clinton was campaigning for at the time.

One of the key ingredients in the ADFA Ponzi formula was the availability of a system of banks that would agree to ignore the strictures of the Bank Secrecy Act of 1970.[30] That law required that CTRs (currency transaction reports) be filed in connection with cash deposits of amounts of ten thousand dollars or more at banking institutions. The CTRs are filed with the Internal Revenue Service, ostensibly in order for the IRS to follow money trails back to their sources, in the event someone conveniently forgot to report cash income. Finding banks that would allow cash deposits sans CTRs wasn't very difficult in Clinton's Arkansas. The Stephens-owned Worthen Bank, the Bank of Kingston, the Perry County Bank, the Bank of Cherry Valley, the Union Bank of Mena, FirstSouth of Pine Bluff, and the Bank of Paragould, among others, knew how to take care of their preferred customers. When the amount of black money sought to be deposited pushed the banks in the network outside of their comfort zones, BCCI was there to take up the slack. Since the drug traffickers, like Barry Seal, were paid up front, those in the ADFA loop got delayed gratification. But, it was worth the wait, since upwards of $18 billion went through ADFA between 1985 and 1992.[31]

With normal bond issues, the beneficiary gets a loan at below-market rates. A bank or other financial institution sells the bonds and gets an underwriting fee. Outside counsel generally makes sure that the deal conforms to law and prepares certain documents required by the IRS, the U.S. Treasury Department, and sometimes the SEC. A second bank or financial institution is then chosen to act as trustee to collect the payments made by the beneficiary. That bank pays the bond purchasers their dividends. The beneficiary also generally hires its own counsel. All normal bond transactions are characterized by detached, arm's-length dealings.

Things were done differently at ADFA. Each bond issue or loan transaction was replete with incestuous relationships and conflicting interests. An example of how far ADFA deals differed from the norm can be seen in the POM transaction. In December 1986, POM was a beneficiary, receiving a $2.75 million loan through ADFA.

POM was owned by Webb Hubbell's father-in-law, Seth Ward. Webb Hubbell sat on the board of POM. Webb Hubbell sat on the board of ADFA. And, as a partner at Rose, Webb Hubbell also acted as closing attorney, certifying that the transaction comported with state and federal law. Between 1985 and 1992, Stephens, Inc., underwrote or sold 78 percent of ADFA's housing and industrial bonds, in spite of the fact that two Stephens executives served on the ten-member ADFA board. All board members were appointed by Governor Clinton.[32] In 1988 and 1989, ADFA loaned $1.37 million to Pine Bluff Warehouse Company. The Rose firm received twenty-two thousand dollars in legal fees to do the loan closing. The trustee was the National Bank of Commerce, of Pine Bluff, a Worthen Bank. The vice president of the trustee bank was an ADFA board member, and the CEO was the father of Rose lawyer William Kennedy III. Bill Clinton later appointed Kennedy to serve as associate White House counsel. Stephens, Inc., was the underwriter for the bonds.

In 1989, ADFA loaned $4.67 million to Arkansas Freightways. Stephens, Inc., owned a large block of stock in the company. Rose did some of the legal work on the loan closing. The trustee bank's executive vice president was an ADFA board member. And, Stephens, Inc., did the underwriting.

In the late 1980s, the investment house of Goldman, Sachs, & Co., helped underwrite some $400 million in bonds for ADFA. According to the Federal Election Commission, Goldman Sachs officers contributed over one hundred thousand dollars to Bill Clinton's presidential campaign and raised millions more. The FEC reported that Robert Rubin, Clinton's assistant to the president for economic development, and his wife had given $275,000 from their "personal foundation" to the Clinton presidential campaign while Rubin was co-chairman of Goldman Sachs. Goldman Sachs also made gen-erous contributions for setting up the Democratic National Convention in New York City in 1992.[33]

While Bill Clinton was governor, Stephens' companies were involved in underwriting or acted as trustees in 61 percent of all of the bond issues in Arkansas through ADFA. When Clinton lost the New Hampshire primary, Worthen Bank gave him a $2 million line of credit. Worthen Bank then became the depository for the Clinton presidential campaign. Fifty-five million dollars in campaign funds went through Worthen in 1992. And, on the eve of the November 1992 elections, the Clinton campaign owed $4 million to Worthen.

With billions of dollars going through ADFA accounts, it isn't surprising that Larry Nichols was appalled to find that principal and interest amounts would accrue over a thirty-day period, only to be zeroed out at the end of the month without any payments being made by the bond beneficiaries. He simply wasn't expecting to find a Ponzi scheme.

The Goring of the Ox

From the CIA's perspective, drug smuggling was an excellent way to conceal its arms-smuggling activities, that is, as long as the right hand and the left hand knew what each was doing. Unfortunately, government agencies, particularly those involved in law enforcement, aren't always the well-oiled machines they hold themselves out to be. In this case, it was the FBI that first dropped the ball.

In 1988, Charles Black was the Polk County chief deputy prosecutor. The unsuspecting Black had been gathering data on strange activities in and around Mena and Nella for years when, in October of that year, he wrote Governor Clinton a letter explaining some of his findings. He explained that he had over twenty thousand pages of documented evidence about what he believed to be smuggling activities in northwestern Polk County, near Rich Mountain. His purpose for writing the governor was twofold. First, he wanted Clinton to know he was serious and had done his homework methodically and carefully. Second, he needed money to carry on an investigation which would be "a joint effort by several agencies, including the Arkansas State Police, the DEA, the FBI, the IRS, and the U.S. Customs Service." In order to complete his investigation and bring the ne'er-do-wells to justice, he figured he would need about twenty thousand dollars. With that he could convene a grand jury, with the governor's permission, and really do things right.[34]

The fly might just as well have asked the spider for a pair of scissors to destroy its web. Needless to say, Clinton wasn't about to throw a dime in Black's direction, but that wasn't communicated to Black. After patting him on the back for a job well done, Clinton told Black he would get twenty-five thousand dollars for his investigation as soon as possible. Black had indicated to Clinton that time was of the essence, so he was naturally excited over the governor's response. He began gearing up for the task ahead, but when November and December came and went and he hadn't heard anything from Little Rock, he contacted Bill Alexander, the congressman who represented Polk County. Congressman Alexander then wrote Clinton in January 1989 and was told the same thing: the money would be coming soon.[35]

To put Charles Black's October 1988 request in perspective, as early as 1984, investigators with the Arkansas State Police in Polk County had reported that a great deal of money was flowing into Arkansas from the gun-smuggling trade. They also knew black money was being laundered through often unsuspecting local businesses and banks. Barry Seal joked about throwing "dope money" around in Mena when he would go into town to buy supplies. The increased flow of cash also led to an IRS CID investigation. The chief investigators with the Arkansas State Police and the IRS CID were Russell Welch and William Duncan.[36]

Welch and Duncan might never have been interested in the extracurricular avocational affairs of a few "good old boys" in Polk County, had the CIA not grown so comfortable in the security of its network. With Bill Clinton turning all the right knobs and pushing all the right buttons, in complete control of a state government that was very user-friendly to its governors, the CIA was safe and secure from all alarm, or so it seemed. But, blunders, like failing to stop good-time cowboys like Barry Seal from throwing black money around in public places, and trusting that hard-core cocaine users like Dan Lasater and Roger Clinton could keep their mouths shut about where and how they got their drugs, can make the most fecund scheme come unraveled. Two or three idiosyncratic gaffes were all that was needed to unleash the full investigative power of the federal government. Consequently, the IRS CID began looking into money laundering, the FBI into gun smuggling, and the DEA into cocaine and heroin trafficking. The Arkansas State Police took the veil and looked into everything else. And, the U.S. Attorney's Office began covering things up so that evidence would never reach a grand jury. Meanwhile, Barry Seal was bribing or attempting to bribe agents with each of those organizations, plus U.S. Customs and the FAA. After all, he had a sizeable investment to protect.

ADFA Goes the Way of All Ponzi Schemes

In the late 1980s, in spite of the influx of hundreds of millions of dollars of CIA and drug-trafficking money into Arkansas, and in spite of the additional $75 to $100 million of CIA money the Clinton administration absconded with, which was clearly outside the parameters of their agreement with the CIA, Bill Clinton's government had an enormous shortfall. Like BCCI in London when the Price-Waterhouse audit revealed hundreds of millions of dollars in liabilities over assets and the Saudi oil barons had to be tapped again for the bailout, the ADFA Ponzi scheme was relegated to doing the same. Not surprisingly, through Jackson Stephens' connections, Clinton was able to borrow the money to cover the shortfall from none other than First American Bankshares (formerly Financial General Bankshares), an institution controlled by BCCI, the Third World bank that maintained accounts for the Medellin cartel, Panamanian dictator Manuel Noriega, and Abu Nidal, the Palestinian terrorist and arms dealer.

Endnotes

1. This law requires banks accepting cash deposits of ten thousand dollars or more to file reports of those transactions with the Internal Revenue Service. CTRs require information such as the name and social security or federal tax identification number of the person depositing the cash, its source, and the time it was received by the depositor.

2. See, P.L. 98-215, Section 109(a).

3. See, transcript of Barry Seal's cross-examination, *United States v. Norman Saunders*, et al., Cr. no. 85-165-Spellman, U.S. District Court, Southern District of Florida, p. 474.

4. Title VIII, P.L. 98-215, Section 108.

5. *New Orleans Times Picayune*, 6 March 1986.

6. Terry Reed and John Cummings, *Compromised* (NY: S.P.I. Books, 1994), 50.

7. Ibid.

8. Ibid., 171; L.J. Davis, "The Name of Rose," *The New Republic*, 4 April 1994.

9. Reed and Cummings, *Compromised*, 171.

10. Ibid.

11. Ibid., 167.

12. However, in their book, *Compromised*, Reed and Cummings present the sum of $18.82 billion. Ibid., 232. See also, John Broder and Roger Ostrow, *Los Angeles Times*, 15 March 1994.

13. L.J. Davis, writing in the 4 April 1994, issue of *The New Republic*, places the amount at $7 billion, based on files that were released at the time.

14. Patrick Matrisciana, *The Book Clinton Chronicles* (Hemet, CA: Jeremiah Books, 1994).

15. Davis, *New Republic*.

16. Drug Enforcement Administration, Narcotics Investigation Report, 12 March 1984, File No. GJ-83-Z001, cited in Matrisciana, *Clinton Chronicles*.

17. Reed and Cummings, *Compromised*, 198.

18. In October 1994, former Mississippi Congressman, Michael Espy, resigned as secretary of agriculture. Espy was under intense pressure from the White House because of the DOA's favorable treatment of Tyson's business operations, and because he accepted gifts and perks from Tyson in return for that treatment.

19. Report of Special Agent Anthony J. Coulson, DEA Office, Tucson, Arizona, DEA File No. GFMO-84-4046, entitled "Debriefing of SMO-84-0019 Re: Donald TYSON Drug Trafficking Organization."

20. Ibid.

21. Report of Special Agent H. Dean Gates, DEA Office, Oklahoma City, Oklahoma, DEA File No. GFGJ-83-9052, entitled "Identification of Associate of Jerry PRIDEAUX."

22. At the witness' request she will only be referred to as "Fran." This statement was given to the author in July 1993, during a visit to Seal's camp and airstrip in Ascension Parish, Louisiana.

23. Matrisciana, *Clinton Chronicles*, 57-59.

24. Reed and Cummings, *Compromised*, 171.

25. Ibid., 230-233, 125.

26. Ibid., 131, 138.

27. Matrisciana, *Clinton Chronicles*, 71-77.

28. Ibid., 94–95.

29. Reed and Cummings, *Compromised*, 475.

30. Title 12, U.S. Code, Section 1001, et seq.

31. Reed and Cummings, *Compromised*, 232.

32. L.J. Davis, *The New Republic*, 4 April 1994.

33. Rebecca Borders and Alejandro Benes, *Insight* magazine, 28 November 1994.

34. Matrisciana, *Clinton Chronicles*, 53-56.

35. Ibid., 11.

36. Edward Jay Epstein, *Wall Street Journal*, 9 May 1994; Reed and Cummings, *Compromised*, 130-131.

Chapter Seven

Old Whitewater Keeps on Rollin'

Red Flags

In the late 1980s, in part due to record collapses in the savings and loan (thrift) industry, Congress felt the need to revamp and improve the machinery used by the federal government that had been in place since the 1930s to monitor and regulate thrifts. The Federal Savings and Loan Insurance Corporation (FSLIC) and its sister, the Federal Deposit Insurance Corporation (FDIC), had been given essentially identical functions under Title 12 of the United States Code. However, by 1986, the FSLIC was bankrupt.

Both the FSLIC and the FDIC were authorized to move in when a thrift or bank was placed in receivership or under the authority of state agencies, usually called banking commissions or finance commissions, which are often run by individuals appointed by the governors of the respective states.

The "progress" of a bank or thrift failure typically follows a pattern. Bad credits which can't be discounted and brokered to other institutions or individuals become "schedule items." Examiners with the Federal Home Loan Bank Board (FHLBB) are supposed to audit files periodically to watch for "red flags," like a significant increase in the number of schedule items. An example of a schedule item is a loan that's technically in default and ready to be scheduled for referral to a foreclosure attorney. For a variety of reasons, from file clerks simply misplacing records to outright fraud and collusion on the part of officers to hide the records, bank examiners aren't always the sleuths the government would like them to be. As a rule, they take a "what you see is what you get" approach. If the institution otherwise has a clean record, the books generally have to look a bit strange for bank examiners to dig any deeper.

If the audits don't turn up any red flags, it's not likely that there will be any requests on the part of examiners or the FSLIC or the FDIC for further information. On the other hand, if the examiners do find problems, they start paper trails, beginning with letters referring the thrift's officers to certain accounts. As a rule, the initial correspondence is a polite warning that there are problem areas that should be the focus of special attention by the officers in charge of overseeing those accounts. After two or three letters, attorneys for the institutions are generally brought in as intermediaries. Ultimately, if the government is convinced that serious problems exist, regardless of whatever assurances are being offered by counsel, a "cease and desist" order is issued.

Financial institutions have plenty of options where bad credits are concerned. The best option sometimes is refinancing if the borrower only needs a little breathing room. That way the thrift gets pretty much what it bargained for, albeit with either a longer amortization schedule, a lower interest rate, or both. Another option is to threaten litigation: foreclosure, if the note is a mortgage or some other type of instrument that lends itself to disposition through summary proceedings; regular process if there's no note, or the note doesn't provide for summary collection. The institution can also accept a percentage of the full amount due, or it can broker (sell) the credit to another institution, or individual, for a percentage of what's due. Of course, when the officers are bent on creating the appearance that things are on an even keel, even though the institution has major problems, they have been known to misrepresent the true financial picture by doctoring books, keeping a true and a false set of books, juggling accounts and credits, and even churning accounts in speculative investments in hopes of hitting the jackpot.

If the officers are honest and things just aren't going very well, the feds will make recommendations to the state banking authorities to consider placing the institution in receivership. Receivership is usually resisted for a plethora of reasons, not the least of which is the very distinct possibility that the officers' resumes and curriculum vitae will be forever marred. With a bit of luck, the deposed CEO of a failed thrift may get a job as a janitor on the night shift at some other bank.

If a thrift is placed in receivership and there are sufficient good credits to salvage something of the otherwise failed institution, what's called a "purchase and assumption" generally takes place. When that happens, the feds step in and try to salvage any good credits that remain. A new name is given to a newly formed institution. The strongest credits are purchased by the new thrift, and a few of the bad ones are assumed. The worst ones are turned over to the government for prosecution in civil suits, generally in federal district court.

Sometimes bankers who run failed financial institutions wind up in federal prison. Sometimes the lawyers for those bankers end up joining them there. And, sometimes those who had certain problem obligations (bad credits) also go to federal prison. In the case of *Federal Savings and Loan Insurance Corporation v. SunBelt Federal Savings Bank, FSB, et al.* [Civil No. 86-9011, Div. "B," United States District Court, Middle District of Louisiana], SunBelt bank president Larry Tullos, bank attorney Sidney Fazio, and borrower Michael Blanton were found to have defrauded stockholders and depositors. All three were subsequently indicted, and after entering plea agreements, all three went to federal prison.

The federal government insures accounts of up to one hundred thousand dollars per depositor in each federally insured institution. If an American citizen has that amount or less on deposit in a bank or thrift that fails, the government reimburses him for the entire amount of his losses. For that reason, in the 1980s when thrifts began to fail—due in large part to the failed economic and fiscal policies of the Carter administration in the late seventies—federal regulators got extremely uncomfortable. They had reason to be uncomfortable. Congress would soon be asked to come up with something on the order of $400 to $500 billion to bail out the thrift industry.

Every single federally insured account at every single FDIC or FSLIC member institution was in danger of being lost in the late 1980s, on into the 1990s. And, every one of those accounts, in the amount of one hundred thousand dollars or less, would have to be reimbursed out of the federal till. To make matters worse, there are those in the legal profession who have unscrupulously taken advantage of the tidal wave of litigation precipitated by thrift failures. Large law firms all over the country have double and triple billed their clients, padded hours, and charged for sometimes nonexistent expenses when representing the federal government in this type of litigation. For a while, in the late 1980s and early 1990s, it was commonplace for two large law firms in the same or neighboring cities to handle the same case. The lame excuse given by regulators was that the lawyers had convinced them that a division of labor between two or three firms would expedite matters and ensure that no stone was left unturned in terms of formal discovery.

However, what was in fact happening in many instances was a duplication of efforts, with a resulting double billing. For example, Firm A would charge a fee for a pleading it prepared. Co-counsel, Firm B, would also charge that amount for the pleading, even though it didn't prepare it, justifying the fee on the basis of having "reviewed" the work done by Firm A. That may be acceptable in private practice where a client has hired two law firms to represent it, has been told ahead of time that the two firms will work on that basis, and has agreed that it be done that way, but it's criminal when American taxpayers are footing the bill and have not agreed to it.

Until the late 1980s, the FSLIC was alone cloaked with authority to handle thrift failures and any litigation related to those failures. At that time, in light of the scandalous activities of certain law firms and the fact that the FSLIC was broke (no doubt due in part to the duplicative billing practices of big law firms), Congress decided to restructure the regulatory machinery. What emerged from the laboratory was the Resolution Trust Corporation (RTC). The RTC was given regulatory authority and also had power that had never been clearly given to the FSLIC—to make criminal referrals for the prosecution of officers and other agents of failed institutions when it appeared to the RTC's investigators that there was sufficient information and evidence on which to base criminal charges.

In the late 1970s and early 1980s, one of the easiest ways for a crook to make a killing at a thrift was through real estate joint ventures and exchanges. Appealing to investors because of favorable tax treatment and appealing to lenders because of the ease with which federally secured funds could be loaned to finance the ventures, real estate was *the* investment to make. Simply put, unethical bankers, especially in rural areas, where bank examiners didn't visit nearly as often as they did in the cities, could obtain inflated appraisals, receive federally backed funding based on those appraisals to make loans, and then split the illicit profits with the borrowers. The U.S. Small Business Administration (SBA) found itself on the receiving end of that kind of fraudulent transaction with increasing frequency in the 1980s.

A cunning banker, a devious lawyer, a treacherous governor, and a powerful law firm hired to deal with bank examiners could be a lethal combination in terms of their ability to damage the legitimate interests of the federal government. Such a combination existed in Arkansas in the 1980s. The extent of the damage done has yet to be fully assessed.

Old McDougal Bought a Farm

In 1989, the RTC closed Madison Guaranty Savings & Loan Association. The Arkansas thrift's failure cost American taxpayers close to $50 million. For several years prior to its closing, Madison had fought its own certified public accountants, Frost & Company, and had held federal bank examiners at bay by hiring the prestigious Rose Law Firm to deal with FHLBB examiners. James B. McDougal, president and CEO of Madison, retained the Rose firm for two thousand dollars per month.[1] Rose lawyers Richard Massey, Vince Foster, and Webb Hubbell all worked on the file, mainly making telephone calls and writing and answering letters from CPAs and bank examiners who were increasingly concerned about Madison's shaky situation.

Overextended, underfunded, and poorly managed, Madison looked more like the crumbling, scandal-ridden BCCI of 1990 than the pillar of the Arkansas thrift industry it held itself out to be. Hubbell, in particular, put quite a bit of time and effort into the Madison case—so much time, in fact, that Whitewater special investigators would later double check his hours and expenses and uncover a few surprises. Incredibly, Rose was later hired by the RTC to sue Frost & Co. Rose, of course, handled that litigation, but not without raising a few eyebrows in the legal community. Conflicts of interest are unethical for lawyers in all fifty states. But, the legal community in Arkansas is a very close knit group. And, no one was going to say or do very much when the former chief justice of the Arkansas Supreme Court was the man being accused of having the conflict.

There was a lot more to the Rose-Madison relationship than meets the eye. In 1977, Rose managing partner Joseph Giroir, Jr., hired Hillary Rodham Clinton, the wife of the young Arkansas attorney general, as an associate. She had been teaching at the law school at the University of Arkansas' Little Rock campus and apparently realized that between her and her husband's relatively meager salaries (compared to what Rose agreed to pay), they were not going to be wealthy any time in the near future. The next year the Clintons joined James McDougal and his wife, Susan, in a real-estate venture called Whitewater.

Bill Clinton met Jim McDougal in 1968. Clinton was still in college at the time and hadn't started law school yet, so he volunteered time with U.S. Sen. J. William Fulbright's reelection campaign. McDougal, a staunch Democrat, ran Fulbright's office in Little Rock. Clinton's eagerness to learn the political ropes impressed McDougal, and he took him under his wing.

After the election, McDougal left politics for a while and began to dabble in real estate, managing properties with his aging father. After his graduation from the Yale Law School, Clinton returned to Arkansas with his new wife, Hillary, and they both accepted teaching positions at the University of Arkansas Law School in Fayetteville.

In the late 1970s, when Clinton began to get the urge to run for office, he and McDougal renewed their friendship. According to Susan McDougal, the two couples were very close and "shared an unbelievable relationship."[2]

In the summer of 1978, Bill Clinton had already been elected Arkansas attorney general and was running for governor. On 2 August of that year, Bill and Hillary Clinton and Jim and Susan McDougal bought 203 acres of undeveloped raw land along the White River in the Ozarks in Marion County near the Arkansas-Missouri border. The land was divided into forty lots. Officially naming their venture the Whitewater Development Corporation, they bought the land from a group known as 101 River Development, Inc. The development company had bought a larger tract and had parceled off the 203 acres for separate sale. One of the officers of 101 was the president of a small bank, Citizens Bank and Trust, in tiny Flippin, Arkansas. Amazingly, Citizens agreed to loan the Clinton-McDougal group the full amount of the purchase price, taking a mortgage on the property for security.[3]

The sale was brokered by Christopher Wade. Wade owned Ozark Realty Company. On 14 October 1980, the Clinton-McDougal group sold the most valuable portion of their 203 acres, tract seven, to Chris Wade and Associates. That tract was the largest and was in a prime location at the junction of the White River and one of its smaller tributaries. As reflected in the public records in Marion County, tract seven was sold for a mere two thousand dollars. However, it was resold the next day to M.T. Bronstad, Jr., for thirty-five thousand dollars. Later on, in 1985, twenty-four of the remaining lots were transferred to Ozark Air Services, Inc. Wade was Ozark Air's managing general partner. The public records don't reflect that any money changed hands on that transfer.[4]

According to Wade, he paid over thirty-three thousand dollars for tract seven, but that purchase price wasn't reflected in the records at the courthouse because McDougal didn't intend to pay taxes on that amount of money. He apparently didn't mind paying the transfer tax on two thousand dollars. Besides, his partners were the governor and the First Lady, who was also a partner in the most powerful law firm in the state, so why should he worry about revenue stamps.

Wade explained the cashless transfer to Ozark Air as a simple exchange of property, which, at the time, if done properly, was tax free (on the federal level). But, Wade further explained that he had had an airplane he didn't need, and the Clintons and McDougals had real estate they didn't want. McDougal apparently intended to sell the plane to Seth Ward, Webb Hubbell's father-in-law and the owner of Park-O-Meter, Inc., which manufactured parking meters, among other things, in Russellville. Ward was also an investor in a real estate deal financed by Madison Financial, a sister organization of Madison Guaranty.[5]

Even though the Clintons may have actually lost money in the venture, there seems to be a lot more to Whitewater than meets the eye. For example, there were at least three checking accounts at Madison in the name of Whitewater Development. One of those accounts, notorious for its huge overdrafts, is alleged by Congressman Jim Leach (R-Iowa) to have been part of a shell game of sorts played by McDougal and Clinton, through which unlawful and unreported contributions were funneled into Clinton's gubernatorial campaign in 1985, and possibly in other years as well. Whitewater's tax records also reflect inequities, including Ozark Air's paying the tax bills for two properties it didn't own. And, months after Clinton, as governor, backed legislation giving International Paper Company (IPC) an enormous tax break, a large tract owned by the Clinton-McDougal venture was sold to IPC. Dan Lasater, the former bond daddy and convicted cocaine trafficker who was pardoned by Clinton in 1990, now lives rent-free in an obscure lodge nestled deep in a seven thousand-plus acre tract of forest land sold recently by IPC to a group owned in part by a partner in the Rose Law Firm.

In March 1984, the FDIC sent a memo to the Arkansas Securities Commission, which plays a role in regulating banks in the state, complaining that Madison Bank & Trust Company, a McDougal-owned bank in Kingston, was trying to conceal its weak condition by moving bad credits to Madison Guaranty, McDougal's thrift. One bad credit, in the principal amount of $45,000, was reflected on Madison Bank's books in the name of Stephen Smith, a former administrative assistant to Clinton during his first term as governor. The memo was actually from the regional director of the FDIC and was considered extremely serious by the FHLBB office in Dallas.[6]

Soon after the memo was sent, special examiners were dispatched to Madison Guaranty. Their written report stated that "the viability of the institution" had been "jeopardized" due to poor management and bad credits. They also warned that an audit, or even a compilation by an honest accountant, would probably show that the thrift was bankrupt. After Lee Thalheimer, who at the time was the overseer of the Arkansas thrift industry, went to Dallas and met with FHLBB officials, he wrote a letter to McDougal echoing the sentiments expressed in the FDIC memo and saying how serious he believed the allegations were. At that point, Madison's real-estate loan portfolio was growing at an incredibly fast pace.

Although the Arkansas Securities Commission could have taken action and shut Madison down (others had been closed for less), through a strange changing of the guard at the top, no action was taken. Lee Thalheimer was replaced during this same time frame by Beverly Bassett, the thirty-two-year-old sister of Woody Bassett, one of Clinton's former campaign finance chairmen.[7]

Webb Hubbell and Vince Foster both worked on the Madison files, but, in actuality, it was Richard Massey who did the lion's share of the work dealing with the bank examiners. Massey was given the task of convincing the FHLBB and the other authorities that McDougal's plans to bring in new money would work the thrift out of the dire straits it had gotten itself into. Those plans included an additional issue of nonvoting stock which would inflate the balance sheet to reflect stockholders' equity, but would not wrest control from the existing owners of voting stock. Beverly Bassett accepted Massey's explanation and plan in a letter dated 14 May. Unfortunately for depositors, but especially for the federal government, the "plan" wasn't implemented, and the thrift failed shortly thereafter. Madison, one of hundreds of failing thrifts in the U.S. in the late 1980s, had, for the time being at least, gotten lost in the shuffle.[8]

Former prosecutor and Pulaski County Municipal Court Judge David Hale was set up as a fall guy by Bill Clinton and another former Arkansas governor of the mid-1980s, Jim Guy Tucker. A Sunday school teacher and former president of the Young Democrats at the University of Arkansas who attended John F. Kennedy's inauguration, Hale got his political baptism by fire in 1979, the year he was appointed to the bench by Bill Clinton. That year, the well-intentioned Hale also set up a private finance company called Capital-Management Services, Inc. (CMS). His idea was that as a federally funded small business investment corporation, CMS could do the types of things in deed that ADFA would one day give lip service to in spirit: give disadvantaged entrepreneurs and minority and female-owned small business endeavors access to credit. Sadly, CMS fell into the web woven by Jim McDougal and the Clintons at Madison.[9]

Hale originally met McDougal when he was president of Young Democrats in Fayetteville. The two connected again in the fall of 1985 through Jim Guy Tucker, Hale's lawyer at the time. Tucker arranged a meeting between Hale and McDougal. Tucker's idea was for McDougal to persuade Hale, under the pretext of needing Hale's help to "clean up" Arkansas politics, to make a series of loans from CMS to various projects. After the meeting, Hale decided to help.

Over the next few years, Hale did what he could. CMS ultimately loaned nearly a million dollars to various entities and individuals at McDougal's request. One of those individuals was Stephen Smith, the former Clinton campaign aid and administrative assistant whose $45,000 loan at Madison Bank was in trouble. The Smith loan from CMS, in the same amount as the principal balance Smith owed Madison, was likely used to retire the Madison obligation and "clean up" Madison's books. At the end of the year in 1985, McDougal returned to Hale with his hand held out, asking for yet another loan of $150,000 for Madison.[10]

Hale was beginning to have serious reservations about these various loans. As his level of discomfort increased and he began posing more in-depth questions about security, McDougal began pointing him more and more in Bill Clinton's direction. McDougal arranged a meeting with Clinton among a row of "spec" houses (pre-constructed to the developer's specifications for sale as-is) at Castle Grande, a residential area McDougal was developing. During the meeting, McDougal asked for $150,000 to be loaned to Susan McDougal's advertising firm, Master Marketing, which was a corporate subsidiary of Madison. According to Hale, the way Clinton and McDougal talked, the deal was already signed, sealed, and delivered. When Hale asked about security, he was told to use a tract of land in Marion County referred to as Whitewater. Hale felt the location was too far away, but under pressure, ultimately made a loan for twice that much, secured only by an endorsement on the back of the draft which simply read, "Guaranteed by Madison Guaranty Savings and Loan Little Rock."[11] Although the money loaned to Mrs. McDougal was SBA backed and guaranteed (SBA loans were limited by law to those who couldn't obtain financial assistance elsewhere), the

McDougals' joint financial statement at the time showed assets in excess of $3 million and a net worth of $2 million, including an unencumbered $400,000 home.

The FHLBB wasn't fooled by the shell games McDougal and Clinton were playing. It started its audit on 28 February 1986, and in March, by way of a formal cease-and-desist order, forced James McDougal to yield management to Sarah Worsham-Hawkins, who had actually overseen the 1984 examination which had initially raised the specter of malfeasance at Madison.

Among the things the FHLBB accused McDougal of were diverting large amounts of money from the thrift to himself and his friends and relatives; using federally insured corporate resources to put together large real estate syndications all over the state, most of which weren't even suitable for their proposed purpose; falsifying the thrift's books to make it look stronger than it was, by shifting deposits and credits and skimming funds from those deposits which he then paid to himself and his friends; and funneling money to pay for his development projects through businesses owned by him or Mrs. McDougal.

After McDougal's defenestration, he offered to pledge his Madison stock to Hale to secure the bad credits. Hale refused after checking the public records at the Pulaski County clerk's office and finding that McDougal had pledged the same stock to Worthen Bank in 1981 when he had borrowed seventy thousand dollars. Hale also discovered that McDougal had pledged the stock again to Worthen a couple of years later in connection with a $142,000 loan.[12] Obviously, all things being equal, if McDougal failed to pay his debts, Worthen would own Madison Guaranty—just as BCCI had done when it took Clark Clifford's stock in First American Bankshares.

In 1993, when the RTC stepped in and began investigating Madison Guaranty again, the handwriting was on the wall for Hale. He realized that the last thing he should have done was trust Jim McDougal and Bill

Clinton, but it was much too late to do anything about it. In early 1994, with his trial in federal district court scheduled to begin, Hale pleaded guilty to two counts of unrelated SBA fraud, over a bogus eight-hundred-thousand-dollar transfer to CMS, in exchange for his testimony in the Whitewater case.

Of particular interest in the CMS-Madison relationship is the timing of the loans. James Ring Adams, writing in the February 1994 edition of the *American Spectator*, points out that, where Bill Clinton's friends were concerned, "the most curious transactions take place in Octobers of even-numbered years, that is, just before elections." Adams gives several examples. In October 1980, Hillary Rodham Clinton got a thirty-thousand-dollar loan on behalf of Whitewater to build a demonstration house on the property. The funds came from McDougal's bank in Kingston, but no such amount appears on deposit in the Whitewater account until two months later. Likewise, in October 1984, Madison carried an eighteen-thousand-dollar overdraft on a Whitewater account. In 1980, Bill Clinton was running for governor. In 1984, he was running for reelection.

In addition to these loans, and further supporting Adams' hypothesis, former Arkansas State Trooper L.D. Brown has said that, in October 1986, Clinton and Hale were meeting in an office at the state capitol when Brown overheard Clinton pleading with Hale for more financial assistance. Brown was a member of Clinton's security entourage at the time and never strayed far from the governor. According to Brown, Clinton "was pressuring Hale" for money, saying "Help us out. We need to raise some money."[13]

Brown, the former president of the Arkansas State Troopers Association, maintains that Hale looked shocked and then dropped his head. This information was given to the FBI in connection with the official Whitewater-Madison investigation. Brown also says that before meeting with the FBI on 6 February 1994, James R. "Skip" Rutherford, one of Clinton's old friends and supporters, met with Brown and pleaded with him not to cooperate with the FBI. It also appears that after Brown's meeting, Rutherford met and talked with senior White House advisors, Mack McLarty and Bruce E. Lindsey, and Clinton campaign official and tenacious protector of the Clinton faith, Betsey Wright, about the Brown meeting. Clinton, McLarty, and Lindsey adamantly deny Brown's statement, but it has a definite ring of truth to it, particularly in light of the other October loans.

The RTC Coverup

Roger Altman and Bill Clinton have been close friends since college. They kept in touch through the years even though their careers took different paths. Altman was an avid supporter of his old chum when he ran for president in 1992. With Bill Clinton's election in November of that year came short lists for cabinet-level and subcabinet-level appointments. Although Roger Altman surely would've been Clinton's first choice for Treasury secretary, he owed a favor or two to U.S. Sen. Lloyd Bentsen of Texas. Altman had little or no clout on the Hill. Bentsen had enormous clout. On the other hand, the position of deputy secretary of the Treasury had even more appeal, because unlike the secretary, a deputy could be more mobile and accessible. Cabinet members have reporters hanging around their necks constantly. Deputies don't, unless there's a scandal.

But, Bill Clinton realized in early 1993 that he would need more help from Altman than he could provide at Treasury. He could certainly help out there, but Whitewater was a big bad bogeyman in Clinton's closet, and at the time, the RTC was the entity that controlled its fate. Altman was thus given two hats to wear. He would serve under Lloyd Bentsen as deputy secretary of the Treasury, and until a more permanent appointment could be made, he would also serve as acting director of the RTC.

Although the first Madison Guaranty-related criminal referral came out of the Kansas City RTC office in September 1992, most of the accusations regarding Jim McDougal's diverting funds from Madison Guaranty to prominent politicians like Bill Clinton, and using Madison money to pay for Whitewater, are set out in the nine criminal referrals made in September 1993 and forwarded to the Department of Justice in Washington. RTC senior vice president William Roelle briefed Altman as soon as the March referral was released. He did the same thing on 27 September when the nine referrals outlining McDougal's activities were released. On 8 October, yet another set of RTC criminal referrals was prepared by the Kansas City office. This time they were sent to the U.S. attorney's office in Little Rock. The first mention of any of these referrals in the national media was 31 October.

RTC investigators in Kansas City, reviewing files culled and copied from Madison's records by FHLBB bank examiners and by RTC personnel after McDougal was ousted, found a pattern. It seems that numerous checks made payable to Madison-related entities had been routed through Whitewater accounts. Laura Jean Lewis, an aggressive investigator who worked with the FBI while investigating thrift fraud in Dallas before moving to the Kansas City office, filed the first criminal referral in September 1992, alleging that Whitewater was part of a check-kiting scheme which drained Madison of some $1.5 million. In her second referral, one year later, she charged that Madison had illegally diverted $60,500 to Clinton's 1984 gubernatorial campaign fund. A few days after she filed the second referral, she was advised that the U.S. attorney wasn't going to prosecute the 1992 referral. On 10 November, she was moved off the Whitewater case. In a February 1994 report, Lewis wrote that her review of records generated over a six-month period indicated that a "majority of the [Whitewater-related] checks" were deposited in accounts to pay off certain personal loans.[14] She believed the loans, amounting to hundreds of thousands of dollars, weren't authorized.

Lewis contends that the "people at the top" at RTC wanted to quash the Madison inquiry. As proof of that, she refers to a tape recording of a conference she had on 2 February 1994 with RTC attorney April Breslaw, a member of the RTC's litigation team who was working on the Madison case at the time. Breslaw has rather curiously denied her own statements to Lewis, to the effect that the byline the RTC brass wanted investigators to take was that Whitewater "did not cause a loss to Madison." Breslaw also told Lewis that "head people" were worried about her work and preferred certain answers to others because they wanted "off the hook."[15]

Once Breslaw discovered that Lewis had taped their meeting and admitted there had been a meeting (she had initially denied even having the meeting with Lewis), she explained her denial this way: "Because I did not believe I made the remarks attributed to me, I denied making them in response to questions asked by some members of the press. I still have no recollection of making them."[16] Thus, in addition to having a flawed character, Breslaw also apparently suffers from acute amnesia. These two maladies are epidemic in the Clinton administration.

In October 1993, the RTC in Washington issued a gag order for personnel working on the Whitewater case. When Lewis refused to obey, she was taken off the case. Two months later, in a memo, she wrote of stonewalls and roadblocks in the Whitewater investigation: It is "beginning to sound like somebody, or multiple somebodies, are trying to carefully control the outcome of any investigation. . . . The beginnings of a coverup may have already started months ago."[17]

In the midst of the turmoil in Kansas City, Richard Iorio, supervisor of investigations in that office, was told that key agency officials wanted to put a stop to the investigation as quietly as possible. Iorio refused and continued full tilt with his work. In August 1994, Iorio, Lewis, and Les Ausen, a senior RTC investigator working on the Whitewater case, were placed on administrative leave.

On 24 February 1994, acting RTC director Roger Altman testified during a Senate banking committee oversight hearing that he had had one brief conversation with the Clintons regarding the Whitewater probe. Later, however, when confronted with a multitude of statements to the contrary from White House staffers, he reluctantly admitted that he had had more than *forty* contacts. As to the one meeting, Altman recalled a brief discussion about the statute of limitations. Every lawyer, and most laymen, know that in the absence of some activity designed specifically to conceal a claim, if the statute of limitations has run, whatever type of proceeding has been brought will be dismissed if the defendant can prove when the right to the claim accrued. For that reason, Altman's acknowledgment that he discussed the limitations period with the Clintons (both lawyers) is a glaring admission that they had reason to be concerned about what the RTC might find out about Whitewater.

After Altman's incredible denial of more than one contact with the Clintons regarding the Whitewater storm brewing on the horizon, Jean Hanson, RTC counsel, was also caught prevaricating. Hers was a bit more insidious, however. When she was confronted, under oath, with Altman's denial of having more than one meeting with his bosses about Whitewater, Hanson failed to refute it even though she knew it wasn't true. Hanson contradicted Altman's testimony that he didn't order her to brief Bernie Nussbaum about the RTC investigation.

Yet more damning was Treasury Chief of Staff Joshua Steiner's diary, which documented numerous meetings and conversations between the Treasury and the White House about Whitewater. April Breslaw may have had a slight, albeit extremely tenuous, basis for contending that she didn't recall her own words spoken to Jean Lewis and recorded on Lewis' tape recorder, but for a man to attempt to deny the subjective veracity of his own diary is absolutely preposterous.

Clinton knew what the RTC charges were in September 1993. Bruce Lindsey had been contacted by Clifford Sloan (yet another White House counsel) and advised of the fact that nine criminal referrals were on their way to Washington. Sloan was also told that they included allegations that Arkansas Gov. Jim Guy Tucker, former U.S. Sen. J. William Fulbright, and James McDougal were connected in some conspiratorial way to Whitewater and that the RTC believed funds from Madison had been diverted to Clinton's campaigns. The Clintons were potential witnesses. The RTC investigation had started in Kansas City, and the White House had obtained the unlisted telephone numbers of the RTC investigators there. It was later discovered that all of this information had been given by Jean Hanson to Clifford Sloan.

Hubbell's Last Hurrah

When Rose attorney Richard Massey wrote his very supportive letter to federal bank examiners in 1989, the gilding of Madison's lily was based mainly on an accounting audit performed by Frost & Company. But, the letter only held the hounds at bay temporarily. Peeking inside the silk purse Massey had created, the RTC's Kansas City office found a sow's ear. In addition to issuing a cease and desist order, which normally precedes a takeover by the RTC, Kansas City examiners made their criminal referrals to RTC headquarters in Washington.

The RTC sued Frost & Company almost immediately after taking over Madison. It was clear that Massey's letter had been based on the accounting firm's audit, so it seemed likely that Frost had either conspired with

McDougal to defraud the FHLBB or had grossly erred in its figures. Based on the evidence in the files, the RTC must have felt litigation was a pretty sure bet. On the one hand, damages might be collected for fraud; on the other, damages for accounting malpractice might be proved.

At some point in the ensuing weeks, RTC attorneys determined that it might be best to hire outside counsel to prosecute the action against Frost, in its capacity as the accountant for Madison. The Rose Law Firm was chosen. Despite the existence of flagrant, textbook conflicts of interest (Rose had worked for Madison with Frost in preparing letters to federal bank examiners, based on Frost's accounting), Rose lawyers failed to properly disclose the conflict to the RTC. Moreover, Webb Hubbell was chosen to handle the case for Rose, and he had purloined the Madison files weeks earlier under the pretext of executing a judgment his father-in-law, Seth Ward, had obtained against Madison months earlier. Hubbell learned a great deal about Madison from reviewing those files. He also sent stiff bills to the RTC, representing hours he hadn't worked and expenses he hadn't incurred, at least not in connection with Madison.

In February 1993, Webb Hubbell, Bill Clinton's closest friend and Hillary Rodham Clinton's former law partner, was appointed assistant United States attorney general, making him officially the number three man in the U.S. Department of Justice, the enforcement and prosecutorial wing of the federal government. In December 1994, several months after Hubbell resigned his post at the Justice Department, he was presented with an open and shut case by Whitewater independent counsel, Kenneth Starr. In the face of overwhelming evidence against him regarding his overbilling and fraud, Hubbell quickly pleaded guilty to mail fraud and income tax evasion. Hubbell had billed more than two hundred thousand dollars in improper expenses to the Rose firm.

On 5 December, the eve of Hubbell's plea bargain, Arkansas real estate appraiser Robert Palmer, of Palmer Properties, Inc., pleaded guilty in front of U.S. District Judge G. Thomas Eisele, admitting that he had made at least twenty-five bogus appraisals for Madison Guaranty Savings and Loan. The appraisals, many reflecting inflated values, were often backdated. Palmer had often worked with Arkansas Gov. Jim Guy Tucker and former judge David Hale. One loan, for $825,000 to Hale, in part made it possible for Hale to loan three hundred thousand dollars to Susan McDougal.

If the key papers documenting the insidious machinations of James McDougal, Bill Clinton, Webb Hubbell, Jim Guy Tucker, and the others involved in the Whitewater scam have not all been shredded by the time independent counsel Kenneth Starr gets that far in his investigation, it's highly likely that heads will roll, even though it's uncertain whose heads and how far. One thing is certain, however; as president, just as he did as governor of Arkansas, Bill Clinton has continued to surround himself with fiercely loyal troops who might even commit murder or stage a suicide or two if it means preserving their power and his.

When all is said and done, the real harm to America from the Whitewater fiasco will not be the $50 million price tag placed on the Madison Guaranty bailout and paid by American taxpayers, it will be the complete abandonment of moral principle by the president of the United States.

Endnotes

1. According to some reports, the two-thousand-dollar monthly retainer was paid directly to Hillary Rodham Clinton, after Bill Clinton came to McDougal one morning and pleaded for money. See, James Ring Adams, "Beyond Whitewater," *American Spectator*, February 1994.

2. Ibid.

3. Ibid.

4. Ibid.

5. Ibid.

6. Ibid.

7. Ibid.

8. *Washington Times*, 18 May 1994.

9. Ibid.

10. Ibid.

11. Adams, *American Spectator*, February 1994.

12. *Washington Times*, National Weekly Edition, Special Report, 12 December 1994.

13. Ibid.

14. *Newsweek*, 23 May 1994; *Washington Times*, national weekly edition, 12 December 1994.

15. *Washington Times*, Weekly Edition, 12 December 1994.

16. Ibid.

17. Ibid.

Chapter Eight

Waco, Texas, February-April 1993

The haunting scenes of the flash fire at Mt. Carmel, the Branch Davidian compound near Waco, Texas, on 19 April 1993, will forever be etched in the minds of a generation of Americans. According to the official reports, three fires were started by the Davidians, who had stored flammable liquids in various locations in the sprawling cinderblock facility. Nearly one million rounds of ammunition were expended as they burst from the intense heat.

Much less has been reported about the events of 28 February 1993, the day four special agents of the federal Bureau of Alcohol, Tobacco, and Firearms (ATF) were killed in a shootout at the compound. The shootout followed an attempt to serve Vernon Wayne Howell, aka David Koresh, with a search warrant. All four agents who died had been in then-candidate Bill Clinton's security entourage during his presidential campaign in 1992. Mysteriously, they were transferred from the Secret Service to the ATF only weeks before being hand-picked for the Waco raid.

Were their deaths coincidental? Or, were they sent to their graves like the loyal Old Testament figure Uriah, the husband of Bathsheba? Do the videotapes from KWTX-TV in Waco belie the Justice Department's official report that the Abrams M1-A1 tanks used to penetrate the compound's walls and shoot CS gas cartridges into the building didn't have flammable liquids on board when the assault took place? Was Koresh really the suicidal maniac that psychological postmortems say he was? These are questions that have been, for the most part, carefully avoided in the official reports of the ATF and FBI, but they beg to be answered.

The following analysis is based mainly on the official reports of the Treasury Department and the Justice Department, which are entitled, respectively, "U.S. Department of Justice Report to the Deputy Attorney General on the Events at Waco, Texas February 28 to April 19, 1993 (Branch Davidians)," (which is the FBI report), and "Report of the Department of the Treasury on the Bureau of Alcohol, Tobacco, and Firearms Investigation of Vernon Wayne Howell also known as David Koresh September 1993," (which is the ATF report).*

Who Were the Davidians?

In 1934, Victor Houteff founded a religious sect known as the Davidian Seventh Day Adventists. In 1935, Houteff started a commune outside of Waco, Texas. After his death, and two failed predictions of the Second Coming of Christ, the Davidians split up. The majority followed George "Ben" Roden, who formed a new sect calling themselves the Branch Davidians. They bought the seventy-seven-acre tract at Rt. 7, Box 47-B, in 1957 and named it Mt. Carmel. In 1987, after an armed con-

---

*These reports will be referred to throughout this chapter without specific references to page numbers, unless a portion is an actual quote. Quotes will be referenced in the endnotes as follows: FBI (_____) or ATF (_____).

frontation with Roden's group, for which he was later prosecuted, Vernon Howell became the undisputed leader of the sect.

Vernon Wayne Howell was born on 17 August 1959 and died 19 April 1993 at the age of thirty-three. He dropped out of school in the ninth grade. Howell legally changed his name in 1990 to David Koresh. The reason given in legal documents filed in court in Waco for the name change is that Howell "is an entertainer, and wishes to use the name for publicity and business purposes."[1] With his chief lieutenant, Steve Schneider, Koresh traveled the U.S., Israel, Australia, and Britain, winning converts in each place and helping arrange for their emigration to the U.S.

Koresh controlled almost everything at Mt. Carmel and in 1989 proclaimed himself "the Lamb of God," who was the "chosen one" to open and interpret the seven seals of the New Testament Book of Revelation. Not exactly a model citizen, Koresh strictly prohibited sexual relations between married couples living in the compound. His followers blindly obeyed, despite the fact that one was a Harvard Law School graduate and another was a former police officer. Koresh had ten "carnal" wives, as he referred to them, several of whom were the legal wives of Davidian men. Koresh had sexual relations with his carnal wives, while prohibiting relations between them and their husbands. According to the FBI, Koresh had sexual relations with girls between the ages of ten and fourteen, some of whom were his carnal wives. However, others have stated that the youngest girl he had relations with was fourteen, and that Koresh asked and was given her mother's permission. (Of course, that's still statutory rape in Texas.)

Preoccupied with the "end of the world," Koresh taught his followers that sooner or later, government agents would come, signalling that the end was imminent. On 28 February 1993, as ATF agents attempted to serve a search and arrest warrant on anyone of lawful age in the compound, the Davidians, who'd been "accidentally" tipped off that the raid was imminent, opened fire on the federal agents. Three hours later, four ATF agents were dead and over twenty were wounded.

Improbable Cause

The investigation of the Branch Davidians actually began in May 1992 when a McLennan County deputy sheriff informed the ATF office in Austin of suspicious UPS deliveries to a Davidian-owned mechanic shop and storage building they called the Mag Bag, located a few miles from the compound. The deputy noted that several shipments of firearms worth more than ten thousand dollars had been delivered to the Mag Bag, which was not a federal offense. But, the deputy also noted a "substantial quantity of black powder, an explosive," which could very well be a federal offense.[2] At any rate, in the eyes of the U.S. attorney's office in Waco, it was enough "evidence" to merit a search and arrest warrant.

Koresh was also buying powdered aluminum, thousands of 7.62 millimeter rounds for AR-15 semiautomatic or M-16 automatic rifles, and hundreds of M-16 E-2 conversion kits used to convert the lower receiver housing of semiautomatic Colt AR-15s into fully automatic M-16s. Koresh used some of the same supply houses that furnished parts to the CIA's arms-smuggling operation in Arkansas in the 1980s. These included Nessard Gun Parts, an Illinois company; Sarco, Inc., a New Jersey company which sold conversion kits in Arkansas and Texas in the 1980s; Olympic Arms, Inc., a Washington retailer; Center Fire Systems, of Kentucky; and Shooters Equipment, a South Carolina manufacturer.

Federal law establishes a tax and registration system for the manufacture, transfer, and possession of certain firearms including, especially, machineguns.[3] The federal Criminal Code prohibits the "transfer or possession of machineguns" unless they were lawfully registered before 19 May 1986.[4] What that means is the only automatic weapon the average American citizen has been lawfully allowed to own since May 1986 is one legally registered before that time.[5] And, anyone attempting to buy automatic weapons lawfully before May 1986 could only do so by registering the weapons with the federal government.[6]

The primary violations of federal law the ATF believed the Davidians were committing were the illegal manufacture of machineguns from conversion kits, which would be a violation of Title 26, United States Code, Sections 5822 and 5061(f), and Title 18, Section 922(o)(1), which makes it unlawful to possess an unregistered machinegun.

In addition to the alleged illegal firearms activities, the ATF had information from a social worker that Koresh was abusing and sexually molesting children at the compound. The probable cause affidavit of ATF agent Davy Aguilera relates that Joyce Sparks, a caseworker with the Texas Department of Protective and Regulatory Services (DPS), had visited Mt. Carmel several times in 1992 but had failed to turn up sufficient evidence of child abuse. Most of her suspicions were based on hearsay statements made by disgruntled former cult members. It should be noted that, among lawyers, the Texas DPS has a national reputation for creating abuse situations where none exist. That's not to say there are no legitimate child abuse cases in the nation's second largest state, but the Texas DPS is the penultimate example of meddlesome bureaucratic self-justification and self-perpetuation. It is notorious for generating "shop talk" (contrived gossip composed of serious, but unfounded conclusory allegations) and then acting as though that talk were true.

One example of this may well be Ms. Sparks' purported last conversation with Koresh, reflected in the Aguilera affidavit, in which Koresh allegedly said, "when my time comes, it's going to make the riots in L.A. pale in comparison."[7] The problem with that statement is that Sparks said Koresh told her that in person, yet her last visit with him was before the L.A. riots occurred in April 1993. The ATF report addresses that inconsistency essentially by saying Aguilera's affidavit was mistaken and that Sparks was actually at Mt. Carmel in April, after the riots. But, which is more believable? The hearsay statement of a Texas DPS caseworker? Or, the statements contained in a federal agent's sworn affidavit upon which a possible armed confrontation was to be based? And, since the agent was likely to be a participant in the armed confrontation, he might be very careful about the language he used in that particular affidavit.

An additional basis for the ATF to accept jurisdiction and attempt to serve the warrants was agent Aguilera's report that several of the residents of the compound had been arrested, convicted, or were under investigation for crimes ranging from fraud to smuggling and narcotics offenses. Other Mt. Carmel residents were illegal aliens or had been formerly convicted for firearms violations.

The ATF Raid on Mt. Carmel

When the plans for the raid on the compound began to seriously take shape, sometime in December 1992, a meeting was called in Houston by assistant special agent in charge, Chuck Sarabyn. The meeting was attended by Phillip Chojnacki, of the Houston office, Ted Royster, of the Dallas office, and William Buford, resident agent in charge of the Little Rock office and coteam leader of the New Orleans Special Response Team. Three other agents from Albuquerque, Dallas, and New Orleans attended. Buford, of the Little Rock office, had planned and participated in a tactical operation of the same magnitude before, when he was in charge of the 1985 siege on the 360-acre Arkansas compound of the white supremacist group, CSA (the Covenant, the Sword, and the Arm of the Lord).

Former Davidian David Block gave a good deal of useful information to the ATF before the raid. His statements were mainly relied on for an understanding of the floorplan of the compound. It had been built in several stages, on a piecemeal basis, and there were no blueprints on file anywhere. Block advised agents of the locations of the Davidians' weapons caches, so they had a good idea of where Koresh might be expected to have additional security.

A couple of days before the raid, the Waco newspaper, the *Tribune Herald*, double-crossed the ATF and released the first in a scathing series of articles entitled "Sinful Messiah," exposing the Davidians' penchant for playing with automatic weapons, abusing children, and blindly following Koresh's gospel of doom and destruction. The article also referred to Mt. Carmel as "Rodenville," a moniker given when Ben Roden's group lived there. Koresh abhorred the nickname. Needless to say, when Koresh read the first story, he was livid. Had that been the only problem, the raid might have proceeded without incident. However, the next couple of days were replete with blunders, one of which blew the ATF's cover.

After the Saturday, 27 February publication of the first "Sinful Messiah" installment, the ATF moved the raid date up one day, from Monday, 1 March, to Sunday, 28 February. Because they had to have emergency medical backup, the local ambulance service knew when the raid would take place. An ambulance service employee tipped KWTX-TV, who sent a reporter and a camera crew to cover the raid.

At 7:00 A.M., on Sunday, 28 February cameraman Jim Peeler was roaming the countryside, looking for the huge Mt. Carmel compound. Peeler claims to have become lost and at 8:30 used a cellular telephone to call in for directions. Incredibly, he claims to have gotten lost again and happened upon a mail carrier, who politely gave him directions.

As soon as the camera truck pulled away, the mail carrier, a Branch Davidian named David Jones, sped back to the compound and alerted Koresh. The Davidians were thus armed and ready when the ATF teams arrived. Agent Robert Rodriguez, who had infiltrated the compound and befriended Koresh, was there when Jones came in and whispered the news of the impending raid to Koresh. Rodriguez needed no invitation to leave. Koresh wished him good luck as he walked out the door.

As planned, the ATF raid teams met at a nearby technical college before dawn on the morning of the twenty-eighth, loaded into cattle trucks, and headed for the compound. They pulled up in front of Mt. Carmel and disembarked, infantry style, just as they had rehearsed at Fort Hood all week, surrounding the four-story concrete block facility. The time was 9:30 A.M. After a brief confrontation with Koresh at the front door, the New Orleans team, including agents Conway LeBleu, Todd McKeehan, Kenny King, David Miller, Keith Constantino, and Bill Buford, scaled the first-floor roof for access to Koresh's bedroom windows. The agents were only armed with 9-millimeter automatic pistols. Each man had three fifteen-round magazines, for a total of forty-six rounds (one round was already in the chamber), yet their intelligence indicated the Davidians had hundreds of automatic weapons and thousands of rounds of ammunition.

LeBleu, McKeehan, King, and Miller were to enter the bedroom from the west pitch of the roof, while Buford and Constantino entered from the east. When the agents reached the roof, especially on the west side, they encountered intense gunfire. Miller was able to retreat over to the east side of the roof. Agents LeBleu and McKeehan were killed instantly. King was shot six times and rolled off the roof. Rescuers couldn't get to

him for over an hour and a half because of the hail of
bullets.

Three agents, including Buford and Constantino entered the bedroom window near the east pitch of the
roof and were fired on by someone near the weapons
cache. Outside on the roof, Miller was dodging bullets
coming through the exterior bedroom wall and from
below, through the roof he was standing on. Agent
Stephen Willis was killed as he took cover behind a van
parked in front of the compound. Agent Robert Williams was killed while providing cover for his teammates
on the roof. Some agents now believe those who were
killed could just as easily have been struck by bullets
fired by ATF agents as by bullets fired by Davidians.

It is extremely possible that agents LeBleu and
McKeehan would not have been killed, and King would
not have been seriously wounded, if they had known
there was an air conditioner in Koresh's bedroom window. The air conditioner was clearly visible from the air
and appeared clearly in every FBI aerial reconnaissance
photo taken before the siege. That it was Koresh's room
was obvious from the statements former Davidians had
made to the ATF. In fact, Aguilera had been told that
the only room with an air conditioner was Koresh's.
Despite the fact that the ATF had this specific intelligence, for some unknown reason, no one bothered to
tell the agents who were to scale the west side of the
building that they wouldn't be able to get through that
window and that they would be stuck on the roof in
open view of second, third, and fourth floor windows.

Numerous references to the potential threat of .50
caliber automatic weapon fire are contained in both the
ATF and FBI reports. What is not specifically referred to
is the fact that both the ATF and the FBI also had
infrared, night-vision equipment. Koresh and his prede-
cessors had apparently ignored state and local building

codes, because the walls of the compound weren't steel reinforced. Consequently, with their heat-sensitive infrared surveillance equipment, the federal agents could, to an extent, see into the building and determine where people were at night. Accordingly, their ability to discern the Davidians habits and movement patterns was enhanced, all of which should have helped them plan a near-flawless raid.

The ATF report, filed in the aftermath of the siege and while the memory of the deaths of the agents was still fresh in their minds, reflects a definite air of disgust and indignation at times over the failure of the ATF's intelligence-gathering team to provide accurate information to the agents who would be physically entering the compound. At page thirteen, ATF director, Stephen Higgins is quoted as saying:

> Significant deficiencies in the tactical intelligence gathering structure, most notably the lack of an agent dedicated to intelligence processing and analysis, resulted in a plan that was based on seriously flawed assumptions.

> Not only were the planners too quick to conclude that a massive mid-morning raid was the best possible enforcement option, but they chose a plan whose window of opportunity was much smaller than they realized. The planners also failed to prepare for contingencies that would arise if that window were missed. Against a target as formidable as Koresh, such errors exposed ATF to grievous consequences.

Finally, summing up his disgust, Higgins wrote:

> They lacked . . . the training, experience, and institutional support necessary for the extraordinary operation they were planning.

> . . . ATF's management never addressed these deficiencies by giving planners a supportive structure to supplement their own experiences.

The decision makers in Washington, Houston, Dallas, and New Orleans had sufficient undercover intelligence to conclude the raid had been compromised. The element of surprise was neutralized by a postman who heard about it from an allegedly lost TV cameraman. Cellular telephone calls, which can be picked up over FM radio receivers, were made just prior to the raid by both federal agents and the TV crew. Some of these conversations discussed sensitive information. Yet, armed with this knowledge, the men in charge tried to emulate the First Marine Division and storm the beach. Unfortunately, the Office of the Assistant Secretary for Enforcement wasn't consulted about the final decision. If it had been, according to Deputy Assistant Secretary for Enforcement John P. Simpson, it would have recommended against proceeding. All things considered, the raid was at best ill-advised, and the decision to proceed tragically wrong. At worst, it was the culmination of a very clever plot to permanently silence four agents.

It's probably asking too much to expect a fox to give a balanced, objective report on the carnage at the hen house he's been guarding. Despite being well documented and having an air of objectivity, the Treasury Department's report is rife with subtle pro-ATF, anti-Davidian bias. The report does its best to cast the ATF in the best light possible and includes copious references to "acts of heroism too numerous to describe," an interesting statement in a report that's otherwise punctuated with the most minute details. There is no doubt that praise for the courageous agents who died and were wounded at Mt. Carmel is condigned. They were good soldiers, following orders. It isn't they who should be censured.

The report also attempts to put the Davidians in the worst light possible, by repeatedly referring to baseless allegations that Koresh was molesting and abusing children; by repeatedly mentioning their .50 caliber machineguns as if every Davidian had one pointed at every passerby; and by reminding us time and again that only Koresh's apartment had in-door plumbing. While some of the ATF's criticisms of the Davidians are warranted, others, like the allegations of Davidians hurling racial epithets at a black female agent, are suspect. Several Davidians were African-Americans, and blacks were as welcome as whites to join the cult.

The ATF maintains that Koresh hadn't registered his weapons, yet there's no mention of anyone bothering to ask him about it. The main reason given for that is Koresh's cloistered existence. ATF team leaders said they didn't think he ever left the compound, which is inconsistent with agent Robert Rodriguez's statement that Koresh often left the compound in his car, and jogged several times a month on the open road.

Another gaffe, which may have proved fatal to four agents, was that although Special Agent in Charge Phillip Chojnacki was briefed before the raid by agent Chuck Sarabyn that Koresh had been tipped off, Chojnacki failed to mention it when he had his last preraid conversation with the ATF's National Command Center in Washington, D.C. It is highly likely that armed with such information, the command center would have aborted the raid.

On balance, it seems clear that the decision to proceed with such a raid, in the face of trustworthy information that as many as seventy heavily armed members of a bizarre cult, holed up in a concrete fortress, would blindly follow the instructions of a ruthless demigod, was irresponsible and inexcusable.

Of course, it's possible that the ATF considered all this intelligence and simply chose to ignore it. The Gun Control Act of 1968 and the Organized Crime Act of 1970 had changed the focus of the Bureau of Alcohol, Tobacco, and Firearms from the glamorous image it carried during the days of Eliot Ness, into that of a law enforcement agency with vast jurisdiction. A former ATF official recently described the bureau's rock 'em-sock 'em image this way: "Given the choice of a peaceable interview and kicking in a door just for the pure entertainment, ATF special agents instinctively reach for the battering ram."[8] The official then added that that type of mentality can create "a situation inviting trouble." We now know for whom the trouble was invited, and it wasn't the ATF.

Hellfire and Brimstone: the FBI Assault

The FBI report begins with the same expression of concern the ATF had about .50 caliber weapons:

> [The] FBI . . . faced an unknown number of men, women, and children who barricaded themselves in a large compound, and who refused to surrender. They were heavily armed with hundreds of weapons, including fully automatic machine guns and .50 caliber rifles, and with hundreds of thousands of rounds of ammunition.[9]

At first blush, that statement appears to be accurate. But, it's far from being definitive. It's what is not mentioned that makes it suspect. To begin with, while it may be true that the FBI didn't know exactly how many people were in the compound, it had a pretty good idea, and the exact figure was discernible because former Davidians were supplying information to government agents, and agent Robert Rodriguez had infiltrated Koresh's little kingdom. In the second place, it might have been possible to estimate numbers of people with heat-seeking infrared surveillance equipment.

Before the ATF conducted its 28 February raid, Special Agent Chuck Sarabyn ordered seven Bradley Fighting Vehicles, based on essentially the same intelligence the FBI had later on. The reason for ordering the Bradleys was their armor plating—.50 caliber rounds couldn't pierce it. Sarabyn knew that. Testing armor plating for impenetrability is easy. The military does it all the time. Yet, both the ATF and FBI reports imply that the ability of any conventional weaponry accessible to them to resist .50 caliber rounds was undetermined.

Rather surprisingly, the FBI decided it needed M1-A1 Abrams tanks to resist "the possible high-powered weapons believed to be in the compound."[10] To begin with, either the Bradleys were .50 caliber proof or they weren't. That information is neither top secret nor hard to ascertain. Second, after the ATF raid, the FBI and everyone else involved knew what weapons the Davidians had. It's absurd to think the Davidians would have failed to use every type of weapon at their disposal when dozens of armed ATF agents assaulted the compound and Davidians were dying inside. The idea that they were holding something back is simply a non sequitur.

To the FBI's credit, it admitted at page 122 of its report that the real purpose of ordering two Abrams tanks for the assault was to "use armored vehicles [tanks] to punch holes and insert gas into the building." Attorney General Janet Reno had decided, as early as mid-March, that the use of tear gas was warranted, based on "historical evidence that Koresh had engaged in child physical and sexual abuse over a long period of time."[11]

After numerous meetings and disputes, especially between Reno and FBI Director William Sessions, about the proof of child abuse, and the use of tanks and tear gas, Reno gave the order on 18 April to proceed with the assault. The FBI began early in the morning on 19 April to roll its guns and troops into position.

The assault began when two M-60 Combat Engineering Vehicles (tanks with booms attached) were deployed to the compound. At 11:45 A.M., a wall on the right rear side of the compound collapsed as a result of penetration by the barrel of one of the tanks. The tanks were poking through the unreinforced cinderblock structure and shooting streams of tear gas in fifteen-second bursts into the building. The children would have suffered the most from this, as scientific reports show they are particularly susceptible to choking and asphyxiation and have been known to suffer second degree burns to skin exposed to the gas. Reno knew this, and so did the FBI tactical team on location at the compound. Despite giving lip service to not wanting to "escalate" the situation, Reno ordered the gas continued after Koresh initially pleaded with the FBI to stop.

One of the main reasons given for the escalation of the assault was that the Davidians had begun firing on the vehicles when they came crashing through the compound's walls. Contradictory statements are contained in the official report about the need for stepping up the pace of the assault. On the one hand, the FBI said it feared for agents' safety when the Davidians began firing. On the other, the report says the agents were all safe inside the tanks, which even the .50 caliber rounds couldn't penetrate.

Fire ultimately consumed the compound and everyone inside. There is no doubt about that. The question is, how and where did the first fire start? According to the FBI report, the first fire started at "12:07:41 central time" on the second floor in the southeast corner of the building. But, the report goes on to state: "Just over one minute later a fire that had already started was detected on the first floor mid-section of the building near the dining room."[12] How did the FBI know the second fire had already started if the first fire began on the second floor? Two-and-a-half minutes after the first fire was spotted, it had increased "to the point of full involvement."[13] A third fire was detected on the first floor near the chapel area fifteen seconds later. By "12:10:00," the fire had spread rapidly through the entire building. The conflagration began and ended in a matter of minutes. At least seventy men, women, and children died in the inferno.

The Thompson Film

In the aftermath of the destruction of the Branch Davidian compound, very little physical evidence remained for detectives and special investigators to scrutinize. Most of the bodies were burned so badly they could only be identified through dental records. The bodies of some of the children and aliens will never be identified because there are no extant dental records to rely on.

One of the lingering questions about Waco is whether it was the Davidians or the FBI that started the fires. Attorney Linda Thompson produced a videotape for nationwide distribution, entitled "Waco: The Big Lie," not long after the incident. The tape very clearly shows flames shooting from a tank after its barrel had pierced the wall on the first floor of the compound. In the video, the tape is reversed and slowed to further enhance the accuracy of the scene. It is crystal clear that the tank penetrated the wall and shot some flaming liquid into the building. Shortly after that, the compound was engulfed in flames.

The FBI's response to those allegations was tautological:

> We have investigated Ms. Thompson's claims and find them baseless. The specific CEV [tank] that Ms. Thompson claims emitted a flame has been identified as CEV-1. The time that the portion of the video showing CEV-1 was filmed is unclear. However, based on an examination of the tape, it has been determined that the excerpt Ms. Thompson selected shows CEV-1 in action near the front door of the building. *However, CEV-1 wasn't in that location when the fire started*; instead it was near the front-right corner, and had backed away from the building at least two minutes before the first reports of smoke.... The infrared tape shows a heat source—the exhaust—at the rear of CEV-1,

but no heat source at the front of CEV-1. [emphasis added]

* * * * *

U.S. Army maintenance personnel who were present in Waco, and who were responsible for CEV-1, were also interviewed and shown a copy of Ms. Thompson's video tape. They could offer *no explanation for the appearance of any fire at the end of the boom [barrel].* Neither CEV-1, nor any other vehicle, was outfitted with any flame-throwing apparatus. . . . We are confident . . . that our findings represent the truth. [emphasis added][14]

These statements present an interesting study in semantics. The FBI never denies the validity of the tape or that a tank which was used in the assault that day appears in the tape, shooting a flame into the compound. A tank was clearly shooting flames into the building. Instead, the FBI carefully avoids the issue. "CEV-1," we are told by the FBI, was "identified" as the tank on the tape. The tank on the tape was in the front of the building. But, CEV-1 wasn't in the front of the building. Therefore, . . . what? There's no logical consistency to those statements. Either a tank shot flames into the compound, or it didn't.

Further, the FBI doesn't deny that a tank was shooting flames into the building. Rather, it says its personnel "could offer no explanation of any fire at the end of the boom." Finally, the piece de resistance: "we are confident . . . that our findings represent the truth." The report doesn't say, "We are confident that no tank present on 19 April 1993 shot any flames into the compound." Wouldn't that be the logical response if in fact no tank did shoot flames into the compound?

In the final analysis, the explanation offered by the FBI may sound remotely familiar because it's the same sort of illogical explanation April Breslaw gave during a

Senate banking committee hearing about denying her own taped statements. She simply didn't recall making those statements.

Perhaps the arson team summed it up best: "The [arson] team concluded that the fire was not caused by nor was it intensified by any chemicals present in the *teargassing* operations. . . . [T]he two methods used to deliver the tear gas were non-incendiary" (emphasis added).[15] No one ever questioned whether the *tear gas* was flammable. And, the issue wasn't whether the tanks were supposed to be equipped that day with flame throwing apparatuses. The questions were, quite simply: (1) Was the film authentic? If so, then (2) were tanks used at the compound? If so, then (3) did a tank shoot flames into the building? Those questions haven't been answered. The book on Koresh and his followers is far from closed.

Some FBI employees were questioning the use of tanks and tear gas throughout the siege. Many doubted the propriety of the FBI escalating the operation once the Davidians opened fire, given that the agents on the assault team were safe inside the tanks. Given the official explanations, their doubts seem justified.

Lords and Ladies

At the time of the 28 February raid on Mt. Carmel, Bill Clinton's close friend, Roger Altman, was deputy Treasury secretary and was instructed to ensure that things went smoothly when the warrants were served on the Davidians. Altman even made a special trip to Waco, in furtherance of his duties, after a briefing on 26 February.

Jean Hanson, deputy general counsel to the Treasury Department, best known for her tenacious refusal to change her testimony to comport with that of Roger Altman's during the Whitewater-Madison Guaranty hearings in Congress, was called on to render legal assistance and advice to the ATF in preparing their official report of the incidents at the Davidian compound in February 1993. In her opinion, the ATF had sufficient evidence for a probable cause affidavit and sufficient evidence on which to base the warrants issued for Koresh.

President Clinton sent Altman to Waco when the raid took place and had acting U.S. Attorney General (Janet Reno had not been appointed yet) Stuart Gerson contact him to give him an update as the raid progressed. According to Gerson, the White House had expressed an interest in staying informed. Gerson advised FBI Director William Sessions of the president's request, early on the morning of the ATF raid. Gerson called Clinton personally at 7:30 A.M. to give him an update, as requested. That was two hours before the ATF attempted to serve warrants on Koresh. During the raid, Clinton received two calls from White House Communications Director George Stephanopoulos, advising him about what was happening. When the raid was completed, the president was again briefed on what had taken place. The president also asked to be, and was, informed of the events of 19 April.

The FBI report explains Clinton's keen interest this way:

> From the very beginning of the standoff the Justice Department . . . kept the White House informed of events at Waco. . . . The President had *prior experience* with a standoff-type situation at Fort Chafee, Arkansas [the CSA siege] during his days as Governor, and he was *familiar with the FBI's procedures* in hostage/barricade situations. [emphasis added][16]

Later on, Clinton submitted the following official written statement to the FBI. Here is one of the more interesting excerpts: "While I [Clinton] was *not advised* of the raid on the Koresh Compound on February 28, 1993, *before* it occurred, I believe I was fully advised of developments . . . *subsequent* to that date" (emphasis added).[17] It seems incongruous that everyone except the president contends that he was so interested in what was happening at Mt. Carmel, before and after the raid, that he asked to be kept abreast of the ATF's progress and even sent his close friend Roger Altman to monitor the situation. As number two man at the Treasury, Altman had almost plenary authority to call the shots. The only people he answered to were Secretary Lloyd Bentsen and President Clinton.

The day after the 28 February debacle, the ATF asked Sessions and the FBI to take over. The request gave rise to a number of high-level meetings involving Gerson (as acting attorney general he was in control of the FBI), Webb Hubbell (as assistant attorney general, he was third in line behind Gerson), Altman, and a number of staff members. Gerson knew Janet Reno was going to be replacing him within a few days, so he turned over the reins on the Waco situation to Hubbell. Within a day or two, Hubbell had been briefed by the FBI's Strategic Information Operations Center.

On 2 or 3 March, Altman returned from Texas and met with White House Counsel Bernie Nussbaum, and presidential advisor Bruce Lindsey, to brief them on his trip to Waco and fill them in on the events of 28 February. Clinton also asked Gerson to stay in touch with Stephanopoulos, Nussbaum, and White House Chief of Staff Mack McLarty, regarding Waco until Janet Reno was sworn in on 12 March.

The first time the use of CS gas (tear gas) in the compound was discussed was on 22 March. The next day, assistant U.S. attorney in Waco, Jim Johnston, wrote Reno complaining about the FBI's destruction of crime scene evidence and of U.S. Attorney John Ederer's nonchalant handling of the situation. Reno responded that she would have one of her assistants, Mark Richard, look into the matter. Johnston never heard from Richard.

On 12 April, Reno had a meeting with Hubbell, Nussbaum, Sessions, and other FBI and White House officials. During the meeting, Reno was briefed on the FBI's proposal to use tear gas. During that same week, while preparations for an assault on the compound, using tear gas, were being made and debated at the FBI and the Justice Department, Hubbell attended a meeting at the White House, in Nussbaum's office, to talk more about the plan. Others who attended that meeting were Bruce Lindsey and Vince Foster.

As he had done in connection with the ATF raid, the president made it clear that he wanted to be kept updated by the Justice Department about what was happening in Waco. That was the reason given for so many meetings involving White House personnel. They would receive information and pass it on to Clinton.

Since first considering the use of tear gas, knowing that women and small children were living in the Davidian compound, FBI Director Sessions was not comfortable with Janet Reno's decision to go forward with that phase of the plan. On 6 March, Sessions had spoken with Gary Coker, a Waco attorney who had represented Koresh in the past and asked whether or not Coker might be able to get through to Koresh. Coker explained that Koresh could be very sincere and believed he might be able to negotiate with the Davidian leader:

> Coker was confident that Koresh was remorseful [about the deaths during the ATF raid]. Coker told Sessions that Koresh had come from a broken home, and described Koresh as egotistical, messianic, and craving attention, [but added] "Koresh is afraid of going to prison."[18]

Despite Sessions' efforts, the decision to use tear gas—which could only be administered in this case by using tank booms to penetrate the thin walls of the compound—was never abandoned.

Reno would adamantly maintain until the end that the use of gas was warranted because there was evidence that children were being molested and abused in the compound. In sticking to her guns, as it were, she had to completely ignore the doubts expressed by Dr. Bruce D. Perry, chief of psychiatry at Texas Children's Hospital and associated with the Baylor College of Medicine, who had examined the girls who had been released between the ATF raid in February and the 19 April FBI assault. Dr. Perry found no evidence that Koresh had had sexual intercourse with children or even young girls, although based on his interviews with them, he thought young girls might have been present when "inappropriate sexual things" were discussed.[19] That's a rather strong opinion for Reno to have overlooked, yet she relied almost exclusively on statements from ex-Davidians who might have had any number of reasons to lie about Koresh and his followers.

In all likelihood, Reno probably ignored some of the intelligence she was provided with because she wasn't too terribly interested in the Davidians' fate. Nearly five hours into the operation, which was escalating by the minute, Reno left the command post in Washington to keep a speaking engagement at a conference in Baltimore. The lame excuse given for her abandonment at this crucial time was that "it appeared that the operation would continue for many more hours." Looking at the situation objectively, hundreds of FBI agents, under Reno's ultimate command, were in a "hot" situation, being fired upon. Dozens of civilians, including the children, were holed up in a concrete fortress under the leadership of a suicidal maniac. And, one raid had already resulted in the deaths of four federal agents and an unknown number of cult members. It was absolutely unconscionable for the person in charge of that type of situation to leave for a speaking engagement. Among the topics of Reno's speech? Child abuse.

Why Waco?

The four ATF agents who died at Mt. Carmel on 28 February 1993, were Steve Willis, age thirty-two, Robert Williams, age twenty-six, Conway LeBleu, age thirty, and Todd McKeehan, age twenty-eight. All four were big men. All four had been hand-picked to serve in Bill Clinton's security detail during his 1992 presidential campaign. Between the fall 1992 election and early 1993, the four were transferred from that Secret Service detail to regular ATF field service.

The ATF had information regarding possible federal firearms violations by the Davidians in early 1992. The McLennan County Sheriff's Office had advised the ATF of some suspicious shipments to the Mag Bag, a prefabricated steel building owned by David Koresh and used by the Davidians as a mechanic shop and storage facility.

The Davidians purchased weapons and M-16 E-2 kits, for converting their semiautomatic weapons into automatic weapons. Some of the kits came from companies operating in Arkansas at the same time the CIA gun-smuggling operation, Centaur Rose, was in full swing. A couple of Davidians had been convicted on drug charges in the past, and some of the ATF's intelligence indicated there might be a drug lab at Mt. Carmel.

In the mid-1980s, when Bill Clinton was governor of Arkansas, a radical cult calling itself the Covenant, the Sword, and the Arm of the Lord, occupied a three hundred-plus acre tract in Arkansas. As governor, Clinton called in the Arkansas National Guard to suppress an armed confrontation involving the cult. The ATF was also part of that operation. Bill Buford was one of the ATF team leaders during that siege.

Allegedly because of his prior experience, Bill Buford was called in from the Little Rock office of the ATF to help arrange the Mt. Carmel raid. The four ATF agents who died at Mt. Carmel were all members of Bill Buford's tactical team.

It was common knowledge in Arkansas when Clinton was in the governor's mansion that he did what he pleased, with whom he pleased, and when he pleased. That's one of the reasons he has had to deal with former law enforcement personnel who know about his extra-marital affairs, and who have been privy to conversations with bankers, lawyers, and convicted drug dealers about everything from ADFA to Whitewater. Some of these men are now saying they were bribed with fat-paying, easy government jobs to keep their mouths shut about Clinton's activities. Others, like Little Rock security guard and private investigator, Jerry Parks, haven't been so lucky.

What, if anything, did McKeehan, LeBleu, Willis, and Williams know about Bill Clinton? Why were they the only ones to die in the ATF raid? Why won't the FBI come clean and explain why the tanks shot flames into the compound? There's no better way to destroy evidence on a large scale than a roaring conflagration like the one that consumed Mt. Carmel. These questions must be answered.

The ATF's explanation that the mission failed because their intelligence was somehow ignored and the tactical team leaders forgot to inform their commanders of the leak is not acceptable. The fact that they sent agents into what they knew was a huge arsenal of hundreds of weapons, including .50 caliber rifles, with 9-millimeter pistols is not acceptable. Janet Reno's lame excuse that tanks were needed because tear gas was needed, and tear gas was needed because children were being abused, is not acceptable. A trained psychiatrist, associated with both a pediatric hospital and a major medical school, did not agree that children were being molested or abused. The only proof of child abuse was the statements of disgruntled former Davidians. Bill Clinton's statement that he wasn't aware of the ATF raid until after it happened, despite having sent Roger Altman to Waco and having received a call from Stuart Gerson, as requested, two hours before the raid began, is unacceptable. The case should be reopened, with particular attention paid to Clinton's activities with the four ATF agents who died at Mt. Carmel. Anything less would be a travesty.

Endnotes

1. ATF, p. 1, footnote 1.

2. ATF, p. 17. Explosives are defined in Title 18, U.S. Code, Sections 841(d) and 844(j), to include black powder. Small quantities (fifty pounds or less) are routinely used in refilling bullets, and are exempt. Larger amounts are prohibited.

3. Title 26, U.S. Code, chapter 53, section 5845(b).

4. Title 18, U.S. Code, section 922(o).

5. Qualified Americans could, until recently, apply for and receive licenses to sell automatic weapons and conversion kits.

6. Since May 1986, the law has flatly prohibited the transfer or possession of automatic weapons not registered before the May 1986 cut-off date.

7. ATF, 30.

8. James L. Pate, *American Spectator*, August 1993.

9. FBI, 2.

10. FBI, 118 (emphasis added).

11. FBI, 215.

12. FBI, 295 (emphasis added).

13. FBI, 295.

14. FBI, 305-307.

15. FBI, 333.

16. FBI, 287-288.

17. FBI, 288.

18. FBI, 131.

19. FBI, 221.

20. FBI, 293.

Chapter Nine

Requiem

In the mid-1980s, there was a staggering amount of criminal activity taking place in Arkansas. The CIA's Operation Centaur Rose was in full swing, even in the absence of ace pilots, Barry Seal, who died in February 1986, and Emile Camp, who predeceased Seal by a year and a day.

The drug trade also helped finance the operations of state government. Bill Clinton had formed an organization called ADFA in 1985, ostensibly to provide bond issues for low-interest loans to fledgling and minority businesses that weren't able to obtain financing anywhere else.

In reality, ADFA wasn't as much a bond factory as it was a microcosm of the notorious Bank of Credit and Commerce International, the world's largest Ponzi scheme. Styled after the Pakistani-founded BCCI, ADFA's true stock in trade was drug money. Through a series of well-connected banks, from Pine Bluff to Paragould, cash from the cocaine and heroin trade could be laundered in the land of opportunity. Ignoring the federal Bank Secrecy Act of 1970, which required the filing of CTR transaction reports by banks accepting deposits of cash of ten thousand dollars or more, the banks in ADFA's "loop" could and did launder hundreds of millions of dollars in "black money." And, when things got uncomfortable for them—when special agents with the IRS Criminal Investigation Division came around asking questions—through the Worthen system they could connect with BCCI offices in the Cayman Islands and elsewhere.

This was big business. The CIA's tithe to the state of Arkansas amounted to nearly $300 million during the mid-to-late 1980s. In addition to that money, Don Tyson seems to have been as hard at work in the drug trade as he was selling chickens. And, Clinton's pal Dan Lasater was the king of them all when it came to cocaine trafficking. He flew his own drug runs to Central and South America.

With so many people and so many banks involved, it was inevitable that rural Arkansas, a land of largely unspoiled natural beauty, would eventually be sucked into the black hole Clinton had created to fund his political rise to the top. Barry Seal had once joked that Arkansas was the only place north of Mexico where a drug trafficker could get a police escort, and he wasn't talking about a trip to jail.

Saline County is in central Arkansas, southwest of and bordering Pulaski County. That made it a likely place for people like Barry Seal to unload cash-crop cargo. Seal and other pilots, some of whom had no doubt contracted with the CIA to smuggle armaments and ordnance to the Nicaraguan Freedom Fighters, were free to bring back whatever contraband they could haul to Arkansas.

"Unsolved Mysteries"

On 23 August 1987, sixteen-year-old Don Henry and seventeen-year-old Kevin Ives were found dead on a Union Pacific Railroad track outside Bryant, Arkansas. According to Larry Ives, Kevin's father, the boys were supposedly killed by a freight train at around 4:20 A.M. Don's father Curtis last saw his son at around midnight on the twenty-second. Don and Kevin had been out for a while and had returned home. Kevin was spending the night at the Henrys'. Don asked his father if he and Kevin could go "shine" a deer. Shining is a method of hunting in which the hunter uses a bright flashlight or some other bright light to temporarily blind and freeze the attention of the prey, making the animal an easy target. Although unlawful, shining is a popular night-time activity for teen-aged boys in rural areas.

Curtis Henry and Don joked about who would clean the deer carcass if the boys killed one. Don grabbed his .22 caliber rifle and flashlight, and he and Kevin walked out the door. Kevin was carrying the flashlight. Don told his father they were going to a nearby bean field where they often hunted. The field was about three hundred yards from the Henrys' trailer. That was the last time Curtis Henry saw his son or Kevin Ives alive.

When the boys hadn't returned by 3:30 A.M., Curtis got dressed and went looking for them. He looked in most of the areas he figured they would have gone, but to no avail. At 11:00 A.M. he was still searching when he was informed that someone had been run over by a train. He checked with the county sheriff's office and gave them a description of the boys and what they had worn when they left the house the night before. The deputy informed him that he had described the boys whose bodies were found on the tracks a little after four o'clock that morning.

According to Curtis Henry, the police investigation was botched from the beginning. Assuming the boys' deaths to be accidental, they didn't rope off the area or do very much at all in the way of serious investigation. When State Medical Examiner Fahmy Malak filed his report, it reflected that the boys had large amounts of tetrahydrocannabinol, the hallucinogen found in marijuana, in their blood. In Malak's words, the boys were "unconscious and [*sic*] in a deep sleep on the railroad tracks under [*sic*] psychedelic influence of marijuana."[1]

Curtis Henry absolutely rejected that hypothesis. Don had smoked marijuana before—Curtis knew that—but he wasn't the type of boy to go off and smoke the twenty to twenty-five marijuana cigarettes Malak said he had smoked. When Malak learned that the boys were known to be "clean," he changed his opinion to "suicide." But, according to Curtis Henry, neither Don nor Kevin had any reason to be suicidal. They were well-balanced boys who enjoyed team sports and outdoor recreation like hunting and fishing. There were boys in Bryant who used drugs heavily, to be sure, but Don Henry and Kevin Ives were occasional users at best. The morning after the boy's bodies were found, Linda Ives, Kevin's mother, was told by a deputy sheriff that her son had committed suicide. She was incredulous.

When the bodies were found, Don's rifle was cast aside in the dirt, as though he had thrown it there. Curtis Henry said Don babied the rifle and always kept it clean and oiled. In Henry's words, "He took very good care of his gun, and loved it almost as much as he loved his dad." It would have been completely out of character for Don to treat his rifle that way. Curtis Henry also pointed out that, from his own experience shining deer at night with Don, "Don would not have even gotten on the railroad tracks to begin with, because hunting for deer at night is illegal and if the train engineer would've seen anybody out that late shining for deer . . . he would've called it in." Curtis Henry said he would have hid himself at the sight or sound of a train, as would Don and Kevin.

At the families' insistence, a grand jury was convened, and the bodies were ordered exhumed. A second autopsy was performed by Dr. Joseph Burton, the chief medical examiner in Atlanta, Georgia. His findings were in stark contrast to Malak's. According to Dr. Burton, Don had been stabbed twice in the back, and the back of his head was crushed with the imprint of a gun butt. Kevin had been severely struck on the side of the head with a heavy blunt instrument—possibly a gun butt. Burton also pointed out to the families that he didn't see any evidence that the boys had smoked marijuana. He attributed that conclusion to an erroneous test run by Malak. He also accused Malak of trying to cover up his faulty findings. Burton told Linda Ives that the ambulance crew had reported very dark blood at the scene, indicating the boys had died long before their bodies were found.

There were many other bits of evidence that apparently weren't reported, including a mysterious green tarpaulin, which the train crew had said was partially covering the boys before they were hit. Three men were also reported to have been in a truck near the scene when the ambulance crew showed up. They said they were from the Alexander Fire Department. But, there was no fire department in Alexander.

For all these reasons, the families pushed for a second grand jury, which found evidence to support the conclusion that the boys had been murdered. They also believed there was evidence linking their deaths to increased drug-trafficking activity in Saline County.

Marvella Henry, Don's wife, thinks several people were involved, including the police. She says this because the police took Malak's opinion at face value until Dr. Burton rebutted Malak's findings. Had they assumed the worst—that the boys were murdered—they might have caught the killers. Larry Ives agreed, in part, but added: "I think the main reason we didn't get a thorough investigation to start with is that there's a big drug ring operating in Saline County and a lot of people in the know are involved, and they didn't want an investigation because they thought it would mess up their little party."[2]

Later on, the parents learned they weren't the only

ones questioning what happened and what the police had, or had not done. Saline County Deputy Sheriff Kathy Carty was horrified when told by Lt. Ray Richmond to treat the death scene like a traffic fatality. She told the coroner it looked like a double homicide to her.

The entire investigation was a concatenation of blunders. First, there was the mysterious tarp. Then, one of the boys' severed feet was left at the scene (Malak never even realized it). Two gold chains were found on the ground. One fit the description of a chain Don owned. The origin of the other was unknown. Finally, in a classic case of investigative ineptness, the officer who took all of the measurements used the train as his reference point each time. The train, of course, pulled away later in the day, leaving no benchmark for further investigation.

Beginning in 1993, Curtis Henry met several times with John Brown, a police officer who resigned in 1994 out of frustration over the investigation of the boys' deaths. Brown found numerous examples of shoddy police work, mistakes, and miscalculations in the previous investigation. Dan Harmon, the county prosecutor in Saline County, gave Brown a hard time in an effort to dissuade his investigation. Brown resigned less than a year after he started working on the case.

However, while working on the case, he turned up some very intriguing evidence. He was told Sharlene "Sharlie" Wilson, a former DEA informant, now in jail in Malvern County, had information about the boys. She said Dan Harmon, the prosecutor, was present when the boys were killed and that they were killed by police. High-ranking officials were said to be involved. An agent with the Little Rock DEA Office confirmed that Wilson was a credible witness.

In February 1994, an FBI agent from Little Rock called Brown and told him they were now working on the case. A pilot met with Brown and advised him that

the area where the boys died was known to drug traffickers. He described the railroad tracks and traffic signal,
both landmarks visible from the air. Brown believed him
because the signal lights had once been where he had
placed them, in 1987, but were no longer there. The
pilot added that then-Sheriff Jim Steed gave protection
to drug traffickers, and that Roger Clinton and Skeeter
Ward, Seth Ward's son, often picked up drug drops in
the area. Before Brown could complete his investigation
he was relieved from working on the file. His resigna-
tion followed shortly thereafter.[3]

In 1990, federal agents arrested a used-car dealer
named Davis Callaway, age thirty-seven, of Benton (the
county seat of Saline County), on firearms charges.
During a hearing in an unrelated case at approximately
the same time, before a federal magistrate, Katherine
Brightop testified that she was told by her former boyfriend, Paul Criswell, that he, his father Finnis Criswell,
Callaway, and another man whose name she didn't know
had carried the boys' bodies to the railroad tracks, covered them partially with a tarp, and left them there.
Callaway had caught them burglarizing his home very
early on 23 August. Believing they were trying to steal
cocaine, Callaway killed them and put their bodies on
the tracks.

Both the Ives and Henry families seriously question
those statements. It doesn't make much sense that a
man—even a drug dealer like Callaway—would beat and
stab two boys to death for stealing his drugs. It would
have been easier and made a lot more sense if he had
left them in the house, hidden the cocaine, and then
called the authorities to report that he had killed them
in self-defense, or for intruding into a personal residence. After all, Don did have a rifle that night. That's
a great deal more believable than killing them in Benton,
and then moving their bodies to a railroad track several
miles away near Bryant. How did the boys get to Benton

in the first place? And, why would a murderer in Callaway's situation bring them back to within a mile of their home? The Henrys' and Ives' theory that the boys saw someone doing something illegal and had to be silenced makes more sense than the Callaway story. The boys' case has been featured on NBC's "Unsolved Mysteries," but nothing has ever really broken the case open.

Silencing the Lambs

Many others have died since Kevin Ives and Don Henry were found on the tracks near the Pulaski County line. Keith Coney, a boy about the same age as Kevin and Don, died in the summer of 1988. Coney mysteriously ran his motorcycle into the rear of a semitractor-trailer rig on Interstate 40 near Benton. Coney's brother was with Kevin and Don the night before they died. Unlike Kevin and Don, Coney had a reputation for being a troublemaker. One police officer has said that Coney's throat had been cut before he jumped on his motorcycle to evade being killed; was chased by another vehicle, and passed out from blood loss before running into the truck.

There is one other link between Coney and the Ives and Henry case: Davis Callaway. Coney was selling drugs for Davis Callaway at the time he was killed. Callaway's daughter had also introduced Don and Kevin to each other.

Douglas Wade "Boonie" Bearden was believed by police to be involved in drug dealing. Bearden told state troopers who were interviewing him two days before Coney's death that he knew something about the Henry and Ives case and thought police were involved in their deaths. Coney's death was ruled a traffic fatality. Bearden has been missing since March 1989.

Keith McKaskle was the next to die, in November 1988, two days after Saline County Sheriff Jim Steed was defeated. McKaskle was found by a girlfriend in his garage with over one hundred stab wounds in his body. He was a bouncer and bartender at the Wagon Wheel, a bar on the Pulaski County line, and a personal friend of Curtis Henry. The forty-four-year-old McKaskle was a one-man information broker. He knew everyone in the area, and they all knew him. He often passed on information he learned in the bar to Curtis Henry. It was McKaskle who told one trusted police officer that County Prosecutor Dan Harmon was a drug dealer.

Keith McKaskle had a reputation for being very intelligent and very tough. He was six-feet, two-inches tall and weighed a trim 205 pounds. His pugilistic prowess was legendary. It was said that Keith McKaskle "could clear out a bar unarmed and single-handed."[4] That made it all the more unbelievable when nineteen-year-old Ronald Shane Smith was convicted of murdering McKaskle. The five-foot, eleven-inch Smith only weighed 180 pounds, and had no reputation as a fighter. Smith was, however, at McKaskle's house when five men, wearing black suits and masks, entered his kitchen, led him into the garage with a gun, and then murdered him. Curtis Henry believes, to this day, that McKaskle was killed because of the information he was carrying about the boys' murders.

In January 1989, Gregorie "Fat Greg" Collins, age twenty-six, was found killed by a shotgun blast to the face, in rural Nevada County. Collins had been subpoenaed to testify before a Saline County grand jury in the Henry and Ives case. He had also joined Boonie Bearden on occasion in burglarizing houses for drug money.

Jeff Rhodes disappeared in April 1989. The twenty-one-year old's body was discovered with a bullet through the head at the Crow Landfill, a garbage dump not far from Benton. His body had been burned so badly investigators initially couldn't determine if it was a man's or woman's body. A nine-year-old boy found the body while scrounging through discarded trash. Rhodes' connection to the Henry and Ives case is not clear cut. Sheriff's deputies investigating his death learned that he had called his father two weeks before his death telling him he had to get out of town because he knew too much about McKaskle's murder and the boys on the tracks.

Others connected to the Henry and Ives case have mysteriously committed suicide. Jordan Ketelsen is an example. In June 1990, according to his girlfriend, he pulled up in a truck in the driveway where she was housesitting and blew his brains out with a shotgun. His body was immediately cremated, without any autopsy, even though questions about the circumstances surrounding his death abound. Ketelsen's father, Ron, was a known drug dealer in Benton at the time of his death. It's also rumored that Jordan had information about the Henry and Ives case.

Whatever, or whomever, Kevin Ives and Don Henry saw that fateful August night, must have been terribly threatening to more people than anyone initially suspected. Could they have witnessed what Barry Seal had alluded to in 1985, when he said that if he ever decided to tell his story, no one in government in Arkansas would be able to hide? All things being equal, it's likely the boys saw some sort of obvious drug transaction, that the deal involved some very high-profile, easily recognizable individuals, and that those who were seen by the youngsters were so concerned about being seen, that they decided the best solution was to brutally murder them.

No accounting of the deaths in Arkansas in recent years, directly or indirectly related to Bill Clinton and his illegal operations, is complete without mentioning Jerry Parks.

Jerry Parks was a hulking giant of a man. A former police officer, Parks had left the force and become a private investigator in 1986, starting his own company. At about the same time, he and his wife Jane and their three children moved into the Vantage Point Apartments in Little Rock where, as the complex manager, Jane had come into contact with Roger Clinton.

All summer long, Jane had to deal with Roger's wild parties, many of which involved his brother, cocaine, and unmarried young ladies. As noted earlier, Jane eventually began documenting the parties and the comings and goings of Bill Clinton, Dan Lasater, and other notorious Arkansans at her husband's request. Jerry Parks thought the record keeping might prove useful if anyone tried to sue his family or bring trumped up charges against them in the future.

During the fall of 1992, Jerry's security company obtained the contract to take care of security and maintenance for the building housing the Clinton-Gore campaign. Apparently, near the end of the campaign, Parks suddenly wasn't getting paid. He confronted campaign administrators, including Dee Dee Myers, and was told that the checks had been released and endorsed. Parks didn't deny that, but his problem was that they hadn't been endorsed by him or his company. After several months of threatening lawsuits and dealing with bureaucratic red tape in Washington, he was finally paid.

For several years, in working off and on for Bill Clinton prior to landing the campaign contract, Parks had maintained files on the governor. He had several reasons for this, not the least of which was that certain clients hired him to find out what Clinton was doing at all times of the day, and mostly the night. His files were copious, and they were kept in a safe place in his house in Little Rock.

Late in the afternoon, on 26 September 1993, as Jerry Parks was returning from a Mexican restaurant with a takeout order, a white Chevrolet Caprice pulled up next to his car. Someone in the car began firing a 9-millimeter automatic pistol at Parks, mortally wounding him. He died later that day. After his death, his house was ransacked, and many of the Clinton files were removed.

Since Parks' death, his son Gary has been on a crusade of sorts to prove that there's a strong connection between his father's death and Bill Clinton's activities as governor of Arkansas.

More Dead

In the last two years, a number of other people with ties to Clinton one way or another, have died mysteriously. Time may or may not tell whether those connections were truly associated with their deaths.

C. Victor Raiser, II, and his son Montgomery were killed in a plane crash near Anchorage, Alaska, in July 1992. Victor Raiser was the former finance co-chairman of Clinton's presidential campaign. Raiser's plane crashed in good weather. It had had a fuel system problem. Raiser was aware of improper and unethical campaign finance activities in the Clinton campaign.

Ed Willey, Clinton's campaign chairman, died in November 1993, of allegedly self-inflicted gunshot wounds.

Herschel H. Friday was a prominent Little Rock attorney who died in March 1994. He was a senior partner in Friday, Eldredge, & Clark and a specialist in corporate law. He taught federal jurisdiction and procedure at the University of Arkansas Law School in the early 1950s. He was on numerous committees and held numerous positions with bar associations at all levels. His firm has represented the Union Pacific Railroad for years. Friday was on Clinton's presidential campaign finance committee, with C. Victor Raiser, II. An excellent pilot, Friday was landing in a drizzle on his private airfield when he crashed. Word has it that his airfield was better than the public airstrips in most small municipalities.

In August 1991, Danny Casolaro, a reporter investigating the Mena-BCCI-Contra-ADFA connections, was found dead in the bathroom of his Sheraton Hotel room in Martinsburg, West Virginia, with his wrists slashed ten times. Casolaro was studying the similarities between the Iran-Contra affair and the Inslaw Scandal.

Kathy Ferguson, former wife of Larry Ferguson of "Troopergate" fame, died of an allegedly self-inflicted gunshot wound in May 1994. Ferguson was a registered nurse, and those who knew her and worked with her at Baptist Hospital absolutely reject her death as a suicide. She was very familiar with Clinton's trysts, having been married to Larry Ferguson when he worked for Clinton. She also knew about conversations Larry Ferguson overheard while working for Clinton. One of those conversations was with David Hale. At the time, Clinton was pressuring Hale to come up with more money from Capital-Management Services, Inc., Hale's lending institution. Larry Ferguson later recanted his story about Hale, but Kathy believed it. She was also a close friend of Paula Corbin Jones, the woman who sued Clinton in federal district court in Little Rock for sexual harassment.

Sixty-one-year-old Florence Martin had worked with the CIA as a subcontractor for several years. She had documents and paperwork, as well as the PIN number for Barry Seal's $1.645 billion account at Fuji Bank in the Cayman Islands. She was found dead in her home in Mabell, Texas, in November 1994, with three gunshot wounds to the head. Seal's Fuji account has since been moved to Guaranty Bank in the Caymans and then to a bank in the Virgin Islands.

Nolle Prosequi

In most states, county prosecutors, district attorneys, and state attorneys general have the authority to convene a grand jury to investigate whether or not there's sufficient evidence to return an indictment, formally charging the offender with a felony. The right to that procedure was so important to Americans after the Revolution that it was included in the Fifth Amendment to the federal Constitution, as part of the Bill of Rights. Of course, each state is free to determine its own rules regarding grand juries. By law in Arkansas, all public criminal offenses are indictable by a grand jury or by bill of information. There is an exception for "public officers." Where they are involved, the governor must approve the convening of any grand jury. "Public officers" include all elected and appointed officials, and many bureaucratic positions.[5] Consequently, county prosecutors had great difficulty when they attempted to prosecute anyone in Clinton's "supply line." As was shown in chapter 6, Polk County prosecutor Charles Black was stonewalled by Clinton himself.

In 1988, Black had over twenty thousand pages of incriminating documentary evidence on all sorts of nefarious and clandestine activities in Polk County. What he didn't have was the money to convene a grand jury. So, he did the logical thing and wrote a letter to the man who had the power both to authorize and pay for a grand jury. Black was assured by Clinton that he would receive twenty to twenty-five thousand dollars to proceed. But, neither the money nor the authorization ever came, despite the efforts of both Black and his congressman, Bill Alexander. Alexander even obtained twenty-five thousand dollars in federal funds for the investigation, but Clinton tacitly refused to allow Black to proceed.

Two names that surfaced frequently during Black's discussions with Congressman Alexander were William Duncan and Russell Welch. Duncan had been an IRS CID investigator for several years and had serious suspicions about covert activities in Mena and in Polk County in general. Welch, an investigator with the Arkansas State Police, had similar suspicions. Between Welch, Duncan, Black, and Alexander, a fairly strong case could be made for convening a grand jury. However, Clinton intervened just in time to put a halt to their efforts when he telephoned Arkansas State Police Col. Tommy Goodwin and essentially told him to call off the dogs.

In 1985, when Duncan and Welch had assembled evidence against Barry Seal's associates and revealed his connections with Dan Lasater, they got stonewalled by the U.S. attorney. In 1987, most of Duncan's testimony was excluded by an obscure application of a procedural rule in a House Subcommittee on Crime. He would have testified of his knowledge of a claim by Barry Seal that a large bribe had been paid to U.S. Attorney General Edwin Meese. Duncan said he didn't make much of Seal's claim, but he was aware of it.[6]

If prosecutors' efforts on the state level can be eviscerated by a governor who knows his power, how much more could a president manipulate the legal system to his and his friends' advantage. That's exactly what has happened since Bill Clinton has been in office.

Judge William R. Wilson was appointed to the federal bench in Little Rock in 1993. At the time, Webb Hubbell was the number three man at the Justice Department. Judge Wilson and Bill Clinton are old friends. Wilson represented both Roger Clinton, the president's brother, and Virginia Kelley, the president's mother, when he was in private practice. The other United States district judge in Little Rock is a former Clinton student, as is Paula Casey, the newly installed U.S. attorney in Little Rock. Casey was handling the cases of Webb Hubbell and David Hale for a year before independent counsel Kenneth Starr's team relieved her of those duties.

When Bill Clinton appointed Janet Reno as attorney general in 1993, one of his criteria had to have been that she immediately fire all U.S. attorneys in every jurisdiction and replace them with hand-picked team players. Roger Altman was quickly chosen as deputy Treasury secretary, the man in charge of the practical aspects of running that department. He would call the shots where the ATF was concerned, and Clinton even sent him to Waco to monitor the events surrounding the 28 February 1993 raid. Likewise, the highly trusted Altman was chosen to head the RTC, the agency that Clinton knew was at the time investigating his dealings with Jim McDougal, Madison-Guaranty Savings & Loan, and Whitewater Development Corporation.

Serving under these men and women were various trusted "company" personnel who wouldn't think of questioning the president's decisions, however strange they might have seemed. Vince Foster was a prime example of that, as was Bernie Nussbaum. All the while, Clinton has been appointing judge after judge to the federal bench nationwide.

The day after the ATF raid on the Mt. Carmel Davidian compound, the FBI was in front of the building destroying physical evidence. The assistant U.S. attorney in that jurisdiction complained very loudly that the new U.S. attorney had a "ho-hum" attitude about it. His complaints fell on deaf ears.

If one word characterizes the Clinton administration, it must be the word *deception*. Clinton is a master of the shell game. A very astute and devious politician, he has a keen understanding of not only the power of his office, but also of the offices to which he appoints his faithful followers.

Bill Clinton doesn't stop with Machiavellian machinations on the political front, he also understands and controls purse strings very well. He created ADFA in 1985, modeled it after the world's largest Ponzi scheme, BCCI, and sold it to taxpayers under the pretext of its being a boon to the existence of those who, but for organizations like ADFA, simply couldn't get started in business. And, that's where Bill Clinton's altruism begins and ends—on paper. Someone is being born in Arkansas right now, and someone else is dying. Hopefully, the one who's dying isn't being helped along by the likes of Bill Clinton.

Endnotes

1. Mara Leveritt, *Arkansas Times*, January 1992.

2. Ibid.

3. Patrick Matrisciana, *The Clinton Chronicles Book* (Hemet, CA: Jeremiah Books, 1994) 103-106.

4. Leveritt, *Arkansas Times*.

5. Arkansas Constitution, Amendment 21; Arkansas Code of 1987, 16-80-101.

6. Micah Morrison, *Wall Street Journal*, 13 October 1994.

We welcome comments from our readers. Feel free to write to us at the following address:

Editorial Department
Huntington House Publishers
P.O. Box 53788
Lafayette, LA 70505

More Good Books from Huntington House

New Gods for a New Age
by Richmond Odom

There is a new state religion in this country. The gods of this new religion are Man, Animals, and Earth. Its roots are deeply embedded in Hinduism and other Eastern religions. The author of *New Gods for a New Age* contends that this new religion has become entrenched in our public and political institutions and is being aggressively imposed on all of us. This humanistic-evolutionary world view has carried great destruction in its path which can be seen in college classrooms where Christianity is belittled, in the courtroom where good is called evil and evil is called good, and in government where the self-interest of those who wield political power is served as opposed to the common good.

ISBN 1-56384-062-6 $9.99

The Best of HUMAN EVENTS
Fifty Years of Conservative Thought and Action
Edited by James C. Roberts

Before Ronald Reagan, before Barry Goldwater, since the closing days of World War II, HUMAN EVENTS stood against the prevailing winds of the liberal political Zeitgeist. HUMAN EVENTS has published the best of three generations of conservative writers—academics, journalists, philosophers, politicians: Frank Chodorov and Richard Weaver, Henry Hazlitt and Hans Sennholz, William F. Buckley and M. Stanton Evans, Jack Kemp and Dan Quayle. A representative sample of their work, marking fifty years of American political and social history, is here collected in a single volume.

ISBN 1-56384-018-9 $34.95 Hardback

The Assault: Liberalism's Attack on Religion, Freedom, and Democracy
by Dale A. Berryhill

In *The Liberal Contradiction,* Berryhill showed just how ludicrous it is when civil rights advocates are racists and feminists are sexists. Now he turns to much more disturbing phenomena, revisiting such issues as censorship, civil rights, gay rights, and political correctness in education and offering commentary and punishment, civil liberties, multiculturalism, and religious freedom. Fortunately, the American people are catching on to the hypocrisy. Still, the culture war is far from over.

ISBN 1-56384-077-4 $9.99

The Dark Side of Freemasonry
by Ed Decker

This book is probably the most significant document ever prepared on the subject of the dark side of the Masonic Lodge. In June 1993, a group of Christian researchers, teachers, and ministry leaders met in Knoxville, Tennessee, to gather together all available information on the subject of Freemasonry and its relationship to the Christian world. Ed Decker brought this explosive material back from Knoxville and here presents it as a warning to those who are unaware of the danger of the Masonic movement.

ISBN 1-56384-061-8 $9.99

Conservative, American & Jewish— I Wouldn't Have It Any Other Way
by Jacob Neusner

Neusner has fought on the front lines of the culture war and here writes reports about sectors of the battles. He has taken a consistent, conservative position in the academy, federal agencies in the humanities and the arts, and in the world of religion in general and Judaism in particular. Engaging, persuasive, controversial in the best sense, these essays set out to change minds and end up touching the hearts and souls of their readers.

ISBN 1-56384-048-0 $9.99

One Man, One Woman, One Lifetime
An Argument for Moral Tradition
by Reuven Bulka

Lifestyles that have been recognized since antiquity as destructive and immoral are promoted today as acceptable choices. Rabbi Reuven Bulka challenges the notion that contemporary society has outgrown the need for moral guidelines. Using both scientific research and classical biblical precepts, he examines changing sexual mores and debunks the arguments offered by activists and the liberal media.

ISBN 1-56384-079-0 $7.99

Hungry for God
Are the Poor Really Unspiritual?
by Larry E. Myers

Inspired by the conviction that the blood of Jesus is the great equalizer, Larry Myers set out to bring much-needed hope and relief to the desperately poor of Mexico. You will be deeply moved by these people, who have so little yet worship their Lord and Savior, even in the midst of their need. You will be inspired by Larry Myers's determination to bring not only medical supplies and food, but light and life to those hungry for God.

ISBN 1056384-075-8 $9.99

The Extermination of Christianity-
A Tyranny of Consensus
by Paul Schenck with Robert L. Schenck

If you are a Christian, you might be shocked to discover that: Popular music, television, and motion pictures are consistently depicting you as a stooge, a hypocrite, a charlatan, a racist, an anti-Semite, or a con artist; you could be expelled from a public high school for giving Christian literature to a classmate; and you could be arrested and jailed for praying on school grounds. This book is a catalogue of anti-Christian propaganda—a record of persecution before it happens!

ISBN 1-56384-051-0 $9.99

Political Correctness: The Cloning of the American Mind
by David Thibodaux, Ph.D.

The author, a professor of literature at the University of Southwestern Louisiana, confronts head on the movement that is now being called Political Correctness. Political correctness, says Thibodaux, "is an umbrella under which advocates of civil rights, gay and lesbian rights, feminism, and environmental causes have gathered." To incur the wrath of these groups, one only has to disagree with them on political, moral, or social issues. To express traditionally Western concepts in universities today can result in not only ostracism, but even suspension. (According to a recent "McNeil-Lehrer News Hour" report, one student was suspended for discussing the reality of the moral law with an avowed homosexual. He was reinstated only after he apologized.)

ISBN 1-56384-026-X Trade Paper $9.99

The Media Hates Conservatives: How It Controls the Flow of Information
by Dale A. Berryhill

Here is clear and powerful evidence that the liberal leaning news media brazenly attempted to influence the outcome of the election between President George Bush and Candidate Bill Clinton. Through a careful analysis of television and newspaper coverage, this book confirms a consistent pattern of liberal bias (even to the point of assisting the Clinton campaign). The major media outlets have taken sides in the culture war. Through bias, distortion, and the violation of professional standards, they have opposed the traditional values embraced by conservatives and most Americans, to the detriment of our country.

ISBN 1-56384-060-X $9.99

High on Adventure
Stories of Good, Clean, Spine-tingling Fun
by Stephen Arrington

From meeting a seventeen-and-a-half-foot great white shark face to face, to diving from an airplane toward the earth's surface at 140 M.P.H., to exploring a sunken battle cruiser from World War II in the dark depths of the South Pacific Ocean, author and adventurer Stephen Arrington retells many exciting tales from his life as a navy frogman and chief diver for the Cousteau Society. Each story is laced with Arrington's Christian belief and outlook that life is an adventure waiting to be had.

ISBN 1-56384-082-0 $7.99

Please Tell Me—Questions People Ask
about Freemasonry . . . and the Answers
by Tom C. McKenney

Since the publication of his first book, *The Deadly Deception*, Tom McKenney has appeared on over 200 talk shows, answering tough questions about Freemasonry from viewers and audiences throughout the USA and Canada. Now, in his latest book, McKenney has compiled the questions most often asked by the public concerning the cult-like nature and anti-Christian activities of the Masonic movement. McKenney tackles topics, such as; Masonry's occult roots; Death Oaths and Masonic Execution; Masonry and the Illuminati; and Masonry's opposition to Christian schools. Tom McKenney warns Christians of all denominations to extricate themselves from Masonic movements.

ISBN 1-56384-013-8 $9.99

Heresy Hunters:
Character Assassination in the Church
James R. Spencer

An alarming error is sweeping the Christian Church. A small, self-appointed band is confusing Bible-scholarship with character assassination. These *Heresy Hunters* fail to distinguish between genuine error and Christian diversity and turn on their brothers in an ungodly feeding frenzy. Jim Spencer suggests that the heresy hunters themselves might be the real heretics, because their misguided zeal risks splitting the church. He calls upon them to abandon their inquisition.

ISBN 1-56384-042-1 $8.99

The Liberal Contradiction
by Dale A. Berryhill

Why are liberals who took part in student demonstrations in the 1960s now trying to stop Operation Rescue from using the very same tactics? Liberalism claims to advocate some definite moral positions: racism and sexism are wrong; tolerance is right; harming the environment is wrong; protecting it is right. But, contemporary liberalism is undermining its own moral foundation. It contends that its positions are morally right and the opposites are wrong, while at the same time, it denies that a moral law (right and wrong) exists.

ISBN 1-56384-055-3 $9.99

Goddess Earth—
Exposing the Pagan Agenda of the
Environmental Movement
by Samantha Smith

There's a new powerhouse in Washington, wielding ominous influence in Congress—it's called the Environmental movement. Its roots are pagan and its agenda is conspicuously anti—Christian. The Environmental movement, says Samantha Smith, is a very powerful force attempting to implement World Government.

ISBN 1-56384-064-2 $9.99

Subtle Serpent:
New Age in the Classroom
by Darylann Whitemarsh
& Bill Reisman

There is a new morality being taught to our children in public schools. Without the consent or even awareness of parents—educators and social engineers are aggressively introducing new moral codes to our children. In most instances, these new moral codes contradict traditional values. Darylann Whitemarsh (a 1989 Teacher of the Year recipient) and Bill Reisman (educator and expert on the occult) combine their knowledge to expose the deliberate madness occurring in our public schools.

ISBN 1-56384-016-2 $9.99

Homeless in America:
The Solution
by Jeremy Reynalds

Author Jeremy Reynalds' current shelter, Joy Junction, located in Albuquerque, New Mexico, has become the state's largest homeless shelter. Beginning with fifty dollars in his pocket and a lot of compassion, Jeremy Reynalds now runs a shelter that has a yearly budget of over $600,000. He receives no government or United Way funding. Anyone who desires to help can, says Reynalds. If you feel a burden to help those less fortunate than you, read this book.

ISBN 1-56384-063-4 $9.99

Inside the New Age Nightmare
by Randall Baer

Are your children safe from the New Age movement? This former New Age leader, one of the world's foremost experts in crystals, brings to light the darkest of the darkness that surrounds the New Age movement. The week that Randall Baer's original book was released, he met with a puzzling and untimely death—his car ran off a mountain pass. His death is still regarded as suspicious.

ISBN 1-56384-022-7 $2.99 (Salt Series)

Out of Control—
Who's Watching Our Child
Protection Agencies?

by Brenda Scott

This book of horror stories is true. The deplorable and unauthorized might of Child Protection Services is capable of reaching into and destroying any home in America. No matter how innocent and happy your family may be, you are one accusation away from disaster. Social workers are allowed to violate constitutional rights and often become judge, jury, and executioner. Innocent parents may appear on computer registers and be branded "child abuser" for life. Every year, it is estimated that over 1 million people are falsely accused of child abuse in this country. You could be next, says author and speaker Brenda Scott.

ISBN 1-56384-069-3 $9.99

Beyond Political Correctness:
Are There Limits to This Lunacy?

by David Thibodaux

Author of the best-selling *Political Correctness: The Cloning of the American Mind,* Dr. David Thibodaux now presents his long awaited sequel—*Beyond Political Correctness: Are There Limits to This Lunacy?* The politically correct movement has now moved beyond college campuses. The movement has succeeded in turning the educational system of this country into a system of indoctrination. Its effect on education was predictable: steadily declining scores on every conceivable test which measures student performance; and, increasing numbers of college freshmen who know a great deal about condoms, homosexuality, and abortion, but whose basic skills in language, math, and science are alarmingly deficient.

ISBN 1-56384-066-9 $9.99

A Jewish Conservative
Looks at Pagan America
by Don Feder

With eloquence and insight that rival essayists of antiquity, Don Feder's pen finds his targets in the enemies of God, family, and American tradition and morality. Deftly . . . delightfully . . . the master allegorist and Titian with a typewriter brings clarity to the most complex sociological issues and invokes giggles and wry smiles from both followers and foes. Feder is Jewish to the core, and he finds in his Judaism no inconsistency with an American Judeo-Christian ethic. Questions of morality plague school administrators, district court judges, senators, congressmen, parents, and employers; they are wrestling for answers in a "changing world." Feder challenges this generation and directs inquirers to the original books of wisdom: the Torah and the Bible.

ISBN 1-56384-036-7 Trade Paper $9.99
ISBN 1-56384-037-5 Hardcover $19.99

Combat Ready
How to Fight the Culture War
by Lynn Stanley

The culture war between traditional values and secular humanism is escalating. At stake are our children. The schools, the liberal media, and even the government, through Outcome Based Education, are indoctrinating our children with moral relativism, instead of moral principles. *Combat Ready* not only discloses the extent to which our society has been influenced by this "anything goes" mentality. It offers sound advice about how parents can protect their children and restore our culture to its biblical foundation.

ISBN 1-56384-074-X $9.99

ORDER THESE HUNTINGTON HOUSE BOOKS !

- America Betrayed—Marlin Maddoux..................................7.99
- The Assault—Dale A. Berryhill...9.99
- Beyond Political Correctness—David Thibodaux.........................9.99
- The Best of HUMAN EVENTS—Edited by James C. Roberts..................34.95
- Can Families Survive in Pagan America?—Samuel Dresner......15.99/31.99 HB
- Circle of Death—Richmond Odom.......................................9.99
- Combat Ready—Lynn Stanley...9.99
- Conservative, American & Jewish—Jacob Neusner.......................9.99
- The Dark Side of Freemasonry—Ed Decker..............................9.99
- The Demonic Roots of Globalism—Gary Kah.............................9.99
- Don't Touch That Dial—Barbara Hattemer & Robert Showers.....9.99/19.99 HB
- En Route to Global Occupation—Gary Kah..............................9.99
- *Exposing the AIDS Scandal—Dr. Paul Cameron....................7.99/2.99
- Freud's War with God—Jack Wright, Jr................................7.99
- Goddess Earth—Samantha Smith..9.99
- Gays & Guns—John Eidsmoe.......................................7.99/14.99 HB
- Health Begins in Him—Terry Dorian..................................9.99
- Heresy Hunters—Jim Spencer...8.99
- Hidden Dangers of the Rainbow—Constance Cumbey.....................9.99
- High-Voltage Christianity—Michael Brown............................9.99
- Homeless in America—Jeremy Reynalds...............................9.99
- How to Homeschool (Yes, You!)—Julia Toto...........................4.99
- Hungry for God—Larry E. Myers......................................9.99
- I Shot an Elephant in My Pajamas—Morrie Ryskind w/ John Roberts......12.99
- *Inside the New Age Nightmare—Randall Baer.....................9.99/2.99
- A Jewish Conservative Looks at Pagan America—Don Feder.....9.99/19.99 HB
- Journey into Darkness—Stephen Arrington............................9.99
- Kinsey, Sex and Fraud—Dr. Judith A. Reisman & Edward Eichel.........11.99
- The Liberal Contradiction—Dale A. Berryhill........................9.99
- Legalized Gambling—John Eidsmoe....................................7.99
- Loyal Opposition—John Eidsmoe......................................8.99
- The Media Hates Conservatives—Dale A. Berryhill.............9.99/19.99 HB
- New Gods for a New Age—Richmond Odom...............................9.99
- One Man, One Woman, One Lifetime—Rabbi Reuven Bulka...............7.99
- Out of Control—Brenda Scott...................................9.99/19.99 HB
- Outcome-Based Education—Peg Luksik & Pamela Hoffecker..............9.99
- The Parched Soul of America—Leslie Kay Hedger w/ Dave Reagan.......10.99
- Please Tell Me—Tom McKenney..9.99
- Political Correctness—David Thibodaux..............................9.99
- Resurrecting the Third Reich—Richard Terrell.......................9.99
- Revival: Its Principles and Personalities—Winkie Pratney...........10.99
- Trojan Horse—Brenda Scott & Samantha Smith.........................9.99
- The Walking Wounded—Jeremy Reynalds...............................9.99

*Available in Salt Series